The Path of Most
Resistance

The Path of Most Resistance

Stories of Mennonite conscientious
objectors who did not cooperate with the
Vietnam War draft

Melissa Miller
and
Phil M. Shenk

Introduction by John M. Drescher

HERALD PRESS
Scottdale, Pennsylvania
Kitchener, Ontario
1982

Library of Congress Cataloging in Publication Data

Miller, Melissa, 1954-
    The path of most resistance.
    1. Vietnamese Conflict, 1961-1975—Draft resisters—
United States. 2. Mennonites—United States. I. Shenk, Phil.
II. Title.
DS559.8.D7M54   959.704'38   82-1060
ISBN 0-8361-1992-4 (pbk.)   AACR2

*To young people who struggle to follow
conscience in times of military conscription*

Contents

Introduction

A s I read *The Path of Most Resistance* I was filled with emotion. These ten stories of young men who took the difficult road, in spite of suffering, because they believed it was the right road, will continue to challenge those who read them in the years to come.

I was deeply moved because I remember so clearly the struggle many such young men had and the struggle parents and the church experienced during the difficult war years. Here were young men, who for conscience' sake, took a radical stance—much too radical for many who also shared their concern for peace and justice. Here also were parents and church leaders who, though in sharp disagreement at times, still sought to stand by and give strong support. As a parent, a preacher, an editor, a part of "the establishment" in the midst of it all I can still sense the emotion, empathy, and excruciating pain of that period.

Certainly there were mixed motives. Who of us can say we have always understood or undertaken everything with purity of purpose or perspective? Some response arose out of guilt over the ease by which peace church young men could get exemption from military service in contrast to those who were conscientiously opposed to war from other groups. Sure there was the rebellion and frustration against "the establishment" by those coming of age and seeking to find themselves. There was the desire to embarrass both the government and church. It was a day of peace marches, sit-ins, and demonstrations and, to be sure, youth were caught up in the currents and causes of the time. There were the deep feelings against the terrible atrocities in Vietnam reported not only in the news, but even more vividly by Christians working in the war-torn lands. And there was the response to conscience and the desire to follow Christ and conscience.

Perhaps parents and the church had taught youth too well that war is wrong, that the way of Christ and suffering is the only faithful way for a Christian to live, and that conscience must be obeyed regardless of the cost. Perhaps parents and the church did not expect youth to take the teaching on peace, love, and concern so seriously.

Many youth felt frustrated because of the refusal of the church to speak out and act in light of all the evils of the war. In an editorial during the sixties, I spilled out my own feelings:

> When I see the incongruity and inconsistency of the Christian engaged in warfare, not only from the New Testament teaching but also from the basic concern man should have for man, I feel that had I a choice between belonging to a church which places its blessing on warfare or to remain outside 'the fold' I would choose the latter. . . .
> When the church will wax bold enough and honest enough and New Testament enough to declare unequivocably its opposition to Christians engaged in killing and destruction; when it will come clear in its call to reconciliation and peace at all points, then the church will again be on its way to both the power and persecution experienced by the early church.

I remember expressing my reaction by writing that the way to stop the war is to change the draft law to include every man over forty years of age who earns more than $10,000. The old and the rich plan and justify wars. I remember writing that, strange as it seems, the two great truths and essentials Christianity teaches, love and peace, are words which cause suspicion in wartime and those who use them or seek to practice them are ridiculed and regarded as traitors, even by the church.

I remember writing that the church has the bloody feet of those who fight instead of the beautiful feet of those who preach the gospel of peace and that the church is so fearful of losing its hide that it has lost its heart.

Anyone who was near the heartbeat of the church during the sixties and early seventies knows that it was a difficult decade. A reactionary mood ran rampant in society with its repercussions in the church. The frustration and fear the nation felt, in its longest war, seemed to rub off in many ways on the church. Everything seemed to be in a state of flux.

In addition there was a clear clash between generations. Many who espoused the radical position of resistance were hard to understand by the older generation because they were often far out in dress, appearance, and other practices which seemed to conflict with other basic beliefs. Many times this bred distrust and doubt as to the sincerity and spiritual commitment of the resisters. Such young people seemed for some to have more in common with hippies than with the household of faith.

The resisters' approach threatened parents and leaders who stood strong for peace in a previous war yet responded by registering and serving as conscientious objectors in Civilian Public Service. It was difficult for many to understand why, when the government provided alternative service, these young men refused to serve and resisted the law. Why rock the boat? It was difficult also for government officials to understand.

But those few who resisted the draft had an influence far out of proportion to their numbers. While some may still question their approach, the resisters helped the church think through its position on peace again. The church, along with these young men, learned that peace is costly, that the church is not always what it ought to be, and that in retrospect some things which are assumed are reaffirmed and others are rejected.

Here then are the stories of ten Mennonite conscientious objectors who refused the draft during the Vietnam war. The reasons for their resistance are shared and the consequences shown—consequences which continue today. Here we notice different roads the resisters took in the face of becoming lawbreakers. Some entered Canada. Some went underground. Others went to jail. Still others served in the hurting spots of humanity.

These personal experiences will serve the future in helping other youth who will face conscription. What can be learned? What should be avoided and what can be aspired to? Here may be help for dealing with other related situations in the future, one of which is the nonpayment of taxes for war purposes.

Here is help for congregations and for denominations in how to deal with differences, how to take commitments seriously, how to be more daring in standing for right when the stakes are high. This book can say much to us who have moved through the sniping sixties and the satisfied seventies into the indulgent eighties. It stands as a record and reminder that some have taken the road of most resistance. There is something for all of us to learn from their example.

John M. Drescher
Harrisonburg, Virginia

Authors' Preface

This is a book about Mennonites who were involved in an intense church skirmish while America was at war at home over the war in Vietnam. It tells the experiences of ten of the more than fifty young Mennonite men who illegally tried not to cooperate with the government's call to arms.

The draft resisters were anomalies among Mennonites, somewhat surprising in a church which has adhered to pacifism since its origins over four centuries ago. The vast majority of Mennonites who were drafted during the Vietnam War took advantage of their legal option to avoid military service. Men who objected to participating in war, on the basis of religious conscience, were allowed by the Selective Service Act of 1948 to enter an alternative service program that furthered "the national health, safety, or interest." Most of the Mennonites drafted in the 1960s and 1970s either entered the church's voluntary service program or worked in salaried "I-W" service assignments to fulfill their draft obligations.

In refusing to take advantage of the alternative their parents had struggled to make legal a generation earlier, the Mennonite resisters tapped a geyser of emotion, criticism, and bewilderment. They became dissidents, even in their Mennonite subculture of religious nonconformity, and evoked common questions from both Mennonites and non-Mennonites alike. Who were these people? What compelled them to take such unusual, extreme action?

Because Mennonite draft resisters represent a chapter of Mennonite history that has been largely untold, we wrote only about their experiences and not of those who entered alternative service. We cast their tales in storytelling fashion, hoping to better convey a sense of how it felt for the resisters and their families to go through the experience, as well as a sense of why they resisted and what happened to them as a result of their choices. Our attempt was to put a human face on this history, to portray the resisters as neither heroes nor heretics, but as normal people living in abnormal times with abnormal convictions.

T he time period covered in this book, the 1960s and early 1970s, were of course tumultuous for all of American society. Under assault were some of the most basic assumptions of the mainstream culture. The escalation of the Vietnam War was particularly volatile. The news media portrayed more and more of the increasingly brutal battle in the jungles of Southeast Asia. The conflict even began to draw blood on America's streets and campuses. As calls for the war to end grew louder, the war seemed to be running even more out of control.

In the crucible of this conflict, a whole generation grew up. Even in their most remote areas, Mennonites could not remain untouched. Mennonites of all ages reacted in ways comparable to that of the broader society. Mennonites were under great pressures—social values were rapidly changing, the results of cultural assimilation were surfacing, and the war and antiwar movements were eliciting sharp emotions. This context made it hard for young and old alike to make sober, well-reasoned decisions.

Some of the more visible of the younger generation of

Mennonites became resisters, implying that the old, accepted way of alternative service was flawed, at least for them. Some of the more vocal of the older generation resisted the resisters, arguing that Mennonite Christians should not challenge the government, and implying that America was right. The flavor of this debate comes out in bits and pieces in the following stories.

This book does not tell the whole story. Any attempt to describe the entirety of the Mennonite draft resisters' experience in such a short space would be failure-prone because of the rich variety of stories. The resisters came from several Mennonite enclaves—Kansas, Pennsylvania, Ohio, Indiana, Virginia. They resisted in various ways and for differing reasons. Some were imprisoned, some fled to Canada, some were sentenced to probationary service assignments, some were not prosecuted, and some were forced to comply by coercion or circumstance.

We hope this collection of stories will help congregations and young people avoid the mistakes and model the virtues of past Mennonite experience. Perhaps the stories will inspire and focus future conscientious objection, serving to improve the articulating and listening, as well as the believing and acting, of people who differ over where to draw the line of conscientious objection to militarism.

The facts upon which these stories are based were drawn from several sources. We conducted oral interviews with each of the ten resisters during 1980. When possible, we also talked with their parents, their families, their pastors, and their friends. To help us capture part of the historical mood, we perused the files of some of the resisters, reading journals, letters, and published articles written by them during their period of draft resistance.

In our preliminary research, we located and surveyed about three dozen of these Vietnam-era resisters and compiled general data on their experiences. From that information, we narrowed the field of story candidates to the ten who appear in the following pages, trying to strike a balanced composite of the rationales, events, consequences, and reflections that existed within the overall experience of Mennonite draft resisters during this time.

To the best of our ability, the viewpoints expressed in each story, and even some of the manners of speaking, are those of the draft resister or his family. However, we take full responsibility for any errors of fact or tone.

This book would not have been written except for the major financial assistance of the Mennonite Central Committee U.S. Peace Section, a grant from the Fraternal Activities Committee of the Mennonite Mutual Aid Association, and the services of Mennonite Board of Missions Voluntary Service. We have arranged for all royalties from the sale of the book to go directly to a fund established by MCC U.S. Peace Section to aid future Mennonite draft resisters.

Dozens of people contributed to this book in a multitude of ways. Special mention must be made of John Stoner who helped to clarify the direction of the book, and to Sara Swartzentruber and the many other typists who labored over transcribing interviews and typing draft after draft of the manuscript. We want to thank those who gave helpful comments on the manuscript, particularly Charlotte Baker, and our many friends and relatives for their gracious, self-giving hospitality, especially that provided by Jay and Shirley Roth. Dean Peachey, Melissa's husband, assisted our project in crucial ways too numerous to mention; his influence can be found on each page of the manuscript. Most of all, we want to thank the ten men and their families who agreed to become the subjects of this book and tell us their stories with openness and honesty.

Melissa Miller
Waterloo, Ontario

Phil M. Shenk
Washington, D.C.

The Path of Most
Resistance

1.

To Jail Is Where It Might Lead

Duane Shank

Duane Shank lives in Washington, D.C., with his wife, Ellen Kennel, and works as the national director of the Committee Against Registration and the Draft (CARD).

He wrote a letter on January 20, 1970, that changed his life. When he dropped it in the mailbox at Eastern Mennonite College, he did not know what all it might mean for his future, just like the time when as a young boy he went up front to get saved at a George Brunk tent revival meeting. He had learned a lot since then about who he was. And a lot about who he wasn't.

But he felt rather grown-up and serious about the decision he had outlined in the letter. For all he knew, it was the most adult thing he had ever done.

He was telling the government that he would not register with the draft system it was using to feed the war it was waging against people in Southeast Asia, people who were his brothers and sisters. He was saying yes to life and no to death. And the government could do what it jolly well pleased with that fact.

Duane had not decided to resist all of a sudden. That was not his way of doing things. There had been one event, however, that probably did set him off in this direction.

It had been back in 1968. He was hardly 16, a thin-framed junior at Lancaster Mennonite High School, in south-central Pennsylvania. "Current Events" was one of his courses, and the teacher, Myron Dietz, encouraged students to form opinions by having them debate each other in class on social topics in the news. Duane's assignment was to argue that the United States was wrong for being in Vietnam.

He had been reading the papers, but in Lancaster, Pennsylvania, the media did not carry much about the war except for proud little news blurbs about beating back communism with the heroic combat valor of local youth, or occasional short notes about weird people putting on antiwar demonstrations in far-off places like Washington, D.C., or Chicago.

His debate assignment forced Duane to go to the library

to read some books and magazine articles. Soon he found himself spending hours reading about what was really going on in the war. Likely because of his diligent research, Duane's side did win the classroom debate—the U.S. should get out.

From then on, the Vietnam War began to consume him. The search and destroy missions. The saturation bombings. The napalming of little children. His concern increased as news of the atrocities mounted. Sure, he played ball, swam, sang in a couple of choruses, and did the usual fun things that young Mennonites do, but he began to absorb the war's pain in unusual amounts.

The thing that bugged him about Mennonites was that they were just content to take advantage of their alternative service privilege and keep quiet about the war. It was so unfair; all a Mennonite guy had to do was get his pastor to help him put down the right answers on the Selective Service conscientious objector (CO) form, tell the draft board he was a Mennonite, and presto, he was working as a CO at a nearby hospital and going home every weekend to see his girlfriend, while other young men were being carted off to shoot and be shot in the jungles of Southeast Asia. What was worse, a CO who was not a Mennonite had a very hard time getting CO status.

D uane felt that if he was to be consistent in renouncing his own participation in war, he also had to oppose everybody's participation in war. The obvious way for him to do that was to refuse to register; he did not want to be part of a system that was forcing people to go to war largely against their will.

So Duane began to do something about it. He talked with Dietz and one or two other teachers at his high school. At church events, he sought out Walt Hackman who worked in Mennonite Central Committee's Peace Section office in nearby Akron, Pennsylvania. He started to get to know some local Quakers at the weekly vigils in Lancaster's downtown Penn Square, joining them in holding up antiwar placards for shoppers and motorists to see. He collected Mennonite Church statements on war and peace. And he delved into the written works of Martin Luther King, Jr., Mahatma Gandhi, John Woolman, George Fox, Jim Douglass, William Stringfellow, Dietrich Bonhoeffer, and others.

Duane felt most alive and creative when he was contemplating the wisdom of these men, all of whom he felt were dealing with the "real" issues of life. For the most part, Lancaster Mennonite High School was stifling for him, its attention caught up in petty regimentation. East Chestnut Street Mennonite, his home congregation, seemed uninterested in an active peace witness. Most of the people around him did not care about the war; they ignored it as best they could. He believed that Mennonites reacted this way because their young men's lives were not at stake.

There was at least one exception to this apathy. Titus Leaman, an older member at East Chestnut Street, vigorously opposed the war in Vietnam. He often spoke up about it in church, put huge sign boards on his car, carried banners at local antiwar vigils, and, at one point, temporarily moved to Canada to protest the federal income tax funding of the war. It seemed that Titus was not taken very seriously by most of the members at East Chestnut Street. But Duane and some of his friends held Titus in high regard. They would sit right up in the front rows with Titus at church, wearing black arm bands to protest the war. They were trying to identify with him, especially since his way of expressing himself was not the typical respectable way for his generation.

After high school, at the age of 17, Duane went directly to Eastern Mennonite College in Harrisonburg, Virginia, in the fall of 1969. There his world expanded like a day lily opening to the sun in fast motion. He was finally with a few people who actually knew what was going on in Vietnam and who refused to sit still and do nothing about it.

The institutional church did not matter much to Duane anymore because it did not concern itself with the important issues. Even the college chapel services, held every morning of the week, were irrelevant. He joined a small group of students in boycotting the required morning chapel services. They did not simply sleep in. They held alternative chapels in the student lounge where they discussed things like the war and activities of the peace movement.

The college administration did not take kindly to the counter-chapel movement and lowered the boycotters' official academic grade point averages for each missed chapel. A friend of Duane's ended up being kicked out of school. Duane ended the year with a huge, negative grade point average, although his unadjusted grades were better than most.

The official penalties simply strengthened the convictions of the antiwar students. The students drew in close, convening many a late night bull session in the dorms or in sleeping bags under the stars, and staging a number of antiwar events. Car loads went over the mountains to D.C. for demonstrations, much to the dismay of college officials. Students' hair grew longer and longer. Blue jeans were their usual attire—cheap, "undressy," and patched. In general, the young worried the older generation a lot.

Seven months of this counter-culture, antiwar atmosphere, and Duane found himself under arrest.

His thin, 18-year-old body squeezed between two FBI agents in the backseat of a gray car cruising down Interstate 81 to jail, Duane could not help asking himself that trite yet suddenly very real question: "Why me?" He had grown up in basically the same kind of home, same kind of church, and same part of the country as had the hundred or so other people in his high school graduating class. Yet he was the only one to refuse to register. "What was different about me?" he wondered. It was a question he kept asking even though he knew it had no answer.

His eighteenth birthday had rolled around just a few months earlier, back in January of 1970, halfway through his first year in college. A handful of his friends, who knew he had been thinking about not registering, had formed a "clearness committee" that helped him ask himself the hard questions about not registering. They had met periodically during the fall of 1969, so that by Christmas of that year he had done about as much thinking as he possibly could have on what he believed and what was possible for him to do about it.

But he still had not finished deciding.

Duane had gone home and spent a couple of nights talking late into the evening with his father, Luke Shank, trying to make Luke aware of how he was feeling and why. It was not that it was all-important for his parents to agree with his decision. It was just that as a 17-year-old, he wanted them to understand why he was doing something like this and at least accept it even if they could not agree with it.

His father tried to make sure Duane knew the implications of this decision and the alternatives. Duane did not learn much that was new to him, but his father's perspective and judgment was something he took seriously. And so, although his father and mother both felt it would be wiser for him to register and go into alternative service like most Mennonites did, they told him that whatever he did, they would stand behind him—it was his decision. This is what he had hoped they would say.

After Christmas vacation, Duane returned to Eastern Mennonite College and prepared his letter to Selective Service. Some friends held a bean soup supper and sing-along fellowship time for him on the eve of his birthday and planned a solidarity march with him to the post office the next morning to mail his letter. But by the next morning it had snowed, and Duane had always thought the march was too big a deal anyway, so they called it off.

Most of his college friends were older than he was. It had been like that for all of his school years. On campus, the people who were concerned about the war were mainly juniors and seniors. They had earlier registered, receiving college deferments. But now their own deferments were soon due to expire or be repealed. They supported his nonregistration inclinations and some of them now had illegally returned or burned their draft cards.

Duane stayed on at Eastern Mennonite College after he sent his letter, doing the usual college student things. He sometimes would go with a group of students down to the southside of Virginia, near Petersburg, to help in a community organizing program. The students would spend weekends leafleting rural neighborhoods, asking people to come to organizational meetings where they could work together as a community on their individual problems.

The southside of Virginia: It did not fit Duane's image of the U.S. It was a rude shock to go from the comfort of white, tranquil Lancaster County, Pennsylvania, to a world of tenant farmers, sharecroppers, and the Ku Klux Klan. That many people actually lived in log cabins with dirt floors and that their children often went hungry was a harsh eye-opener for him.

In the life of a poor, black, sharecropping family, the immediate day-to-day problem was not the war in Vietnam—it was the combination of poverty and racism. But the war abroad and the injustices at home were linked in the minds of the community organizers, and their work caught Duane's imagination.

Yet the black attorney who headed up the community organizing program could not understand why Duane was risking imprisonment by not registering. Other Mennonites had served their alternative service with the project. Duane was a good friend of his and a good worker; the attorney did not want to lose him. He kept trying to convince Duane to register and go into voluntary service, so that he could do some good for people rather than rot away in a cell somewhere, destroying himself for some foolish morality.

Back at Eastern Mennonite College, it did not take long for Selective Service to answer his January letter. This is the law, this is the penalty, and no doubt you have had second thoughts about not registering, so you had better register now or else, read the letter from the Pennsylvania division of Selective Service.

There was also another response—this one a letter from a federal-level assistant attorney general who rambled over two pages as he tried to explain that ours is a society governed by laws, not men, and that each law had to be obeyed or else all laws were undermined and, along with them, all of society. Not very persuasive, Duane thought, but interesting.

Then, in the middle of March 1970, an FBI man tracked Duane down at Eastern Mennonite College, surprising Duane as he padded down his dorm hallway, returning to his room after taking a shower. They moved inside Duane's room, where the agent made sure he was the Duane Shank who had mailed the letter refusing to register, and asked Duane why he had done it. That was all there was this time, but it was clear there would soon be another visit.

Duane began talking with some of his friends about how they might together raise some public attention when the arrest took place. He hoped to stage some sort of big event. Others in the draft-resistance movement were doing "sanctuary" type things—a group of people would surround the fugitive in non-violent protest, forcing the arresting officers to wade through a community of demonstrators in order to arrest their suspect. Duane thought about doing this in a class if the FBI came looking for him, making them walk into the middle of the classroom to haul him out, thus giving him a chance to stand up and proclaim to everybody what was going on. His plans were made in vain; he was outfoxed by the government and, he had a sneaking suspicion, the college administration as well.

He had stayed up most of a mid-April night studying for an exam, and had strolled across the wet morning grass to the chapel building where students in the large class were settling into their seats all primed and ready to be examined. The tests were handed out, quiet descended, and memories began to divulge their crammed responses.

Silently, one of the teachers came forward from the rear of the auditorium and tapped Duane on the arm, whispering that there was someone in the back who wanted to talk to him. Mystified, he got up and walked out, leaving his books and papers lying in his seat. He thought it was a friend needing to know something or a phone call or whatever.

He pushed open the vestibule door and two men in dark business suits stepped up to him, flipped open their badges like they do on TV, asked him if he was Duane Shank, and said, "You're under arrest." In about five seconds he was out the door by the crook of his arms and into the FBI car. Not another soul knew what had happened, except perhaps the professor.

Caught by surprise, Duane's hopes remained just hopes; the whole arrest was disappointingly undramatic. But the rest of the arrest process was rather funny.

The first stop was at the Harrisonburg, Virginia, jail for finger-printing and a mug shot. But that little prison was not deemed secure enough for a federal prisoner like him and since they had to go on down to the federal commissioner's office in Staunton to set bail anyway, they headed for the jail at Waynesboro.

The commissioner in Staunton turned out to be a senile, used-car salesman who, bewildered by it all, let the FBI agents tell him what to do, where to sign, and how high to set the bail. Duane spent a couple of hours in the jail, waiting until Jerry Shenk, a friend of his who was the dean of men at Eastern Mennonite College, gathered together $500 in bail funds and drove down to get him out.

As he sat in the cell waiting on Jerry, Duane figured out that this was only the first step in what would probably be a long, complicated process. There would be an arraignment in which the judge would hear the charge against him and his initial plea. Then there would be a trial. And then, unless he was found innocent, he would be sentenced, probably to jail.

Jail. He had been thinking about it for quite some time. This was it. It seemed rather frightening. He was a little scared of what it would mean in the longer term. Yet, as he wrote to some friends when he got back to campus later that day, to jail is where a life of radical action often leads.

Later that spring, when he left college at term's end, he had a hunch that he would not be back. He might soon be in jail. If not, he felt that doing things in the antiwar movement was more important than staying in school at that point. So he went home to Pennsylvania. To save up some money, he worked for a bit with a landscaping firm and then landed a sweaty job at an iron foundry in nearby Salunga.

His home congregation, East Chestnut Street Mennonite, did not really seem to take much notice of Duane's non-cooperation with the draft. He had been away a year at college. And when he was home, he went to the nearby Lancaster Friends Meeting as often as he showed up at East Chestnut Street. Nevertheless, the members in Duane's congregation were somewhat upset. Everybody knew from the newspapers that he had been arrested. They were shocked or embarrassed about it, but they did not seem to know exactly what to say to him, so they said nothing. However, the congregation did ask him to give a short talk one Sunday morning to explain what he was doing and why. He also spent an evening talking with a small fellowship group his parents were part of in the church.

The work down in rural Virginia still fascinated him. At summer's end in 1970, he hitched to the southside of Virginia to see what it would be like to volunteer there full time. A good friend was working there and the organizing appealed to Duane's sense of service. He stayed a month until he had to leave to go to his arraignment in Philadelphia.

The Friday before Duane's arraignment, the Shanks suddenly found out they had to have $700 to pay the attorney by Monday morning. They did not have it, and were laying plans to borrow it first thing Monday morning. Somehow the word got around and his parents' small fellowship group came up with the cash by the end of the weekend. That surprised Duane. He did not know the church people felt that close to him or his convictions. Maybe they did care; he had been out of contact.

The arraignment itself was so short it seemed unreal. In

about two minutes the clerk of the court read the charge against him and asked him how he pleaded. Duane pleaded not guilty because he did not think he had done anything wrong that he should feel guilty about. And then it was all over until the trial, which was set for January 1971.

About 10 of the 16 people before the court on Duane's arraignment day were there on charges related to draft resistance. Seeing them beside him in the front of the courtroom gave him a sense of strength and camaraderie; they just might be able to fill the courts and the jails and stop this war after all, he hoped.

After the arraignment in the fall of 1970, he hit the road. He squatted down in Goshen, Indiana, for a while, helping to put together a few issues of the Mennonite Draft Resisters' newsletter with some students at the Mennonite college in Goshen, Indiana. He thumbed a ride to do some volunteer work again down in southern Virginia. And he hitchhiked around to several Mennonite gatherings and some caucuses convened by radical Christians at secular peace movement meetings.

The people in the Mennonite-Quaker peace movement were all older than he was. They were part of a loose community of people who understood themselves to be trying to discover new ways of interpreting and moving old truths into present struggles—making Christianity relevant to what was going on in the world. They saw the established church as more a part of the problem than a part of the solution. But they believed it did not have to stay that way.

While waiting for his trial to come up, Duane wrote in a journal entry to himself, "The history of the Christian church has been one of death and persecution. The early Christians died rather than place a pinch of incense on an altar to Caesar. My Anabaptist ancestors lived underground in fear of death and imprisonment. But now the Christian church, and more painful for me, largely the Mennonite church, has become affluent and, as a result, complacent.

"Today's Christians are the politicians who make wars, businessmen who supply them, and taxpayers who support them. Christians have given Caesar more than just a pinch of incense. They have given their money and their lives into its service. Those who are seriously trying to live a Christian life following a God of love and peace as exemplified in Christ are harassed and imprisoned by the 'Christians of America.' "

Duane was on the road, traveling from place to place during this time: talking at churches or on campuses or just visiting with friends. He had close relationships with a few of the people who worked in the peace offices of the church, but in general he felt alienated from Mennonites who were not part of his generation.

He appreciated the official support that the Mennonite Church gave to noncooperators when it produced a statement acknowledging noncooperation with the draft to be a valid option for COs at its Turner, Oregon, conference in 1969. But he sensed that most Mennonites thought people like him were rocking the boat, imperiling the alternative service privilege the church had worked so hard to get during World War II.

Frankly, if people thought he was causing unnecessary trouble that could make it hard for the rest of the Mennonite young men of fighting age, Duane did not care. He told them that it simply should not be easy to avoid and ignore the war. He did not feel he was better than those who had taken the CO route. He just thought people should be serious about it and do what they felt led to do. He happened to feel led to resist registration; he could not participate in the conscription machinery that was feeding bodies to the war, nor could he do alternative service while another less-privileged young man fought in his stead.

While on the road visiting friends, Duane spent a good deal of time refining his beliefs, trying to figure out what he felt was right, testing himself as he waited for the court wheels to turn. He also talked with older war resisters, like David Dellinger, who had spent time in jail for their actions. Duane wanted to know what jail was like, to make sure he could take it if it came to that.

Like Duane, many of his friends were on the road a lot too, and they would often stop over at the Shank home in Lancaster. It became a kind of peace movement hostel. Late night calls from turnpike exits asking for a place to sleep were frequent. The travelers came in twos and fours and sometimes even groups of ten—friends from Eastern Mennonite College, Goshen College, and other places. The backyard and living-room floor of the Shank household were sometimes crowded, especially around the time of Duane's court dates.

Duane's parents were not really put off by the bare feet, blue jeans, long hair, or guitars. That was just the way things were; one just tried not to think about it too much. Many of his friends turned out to be the sons and daughters of church leaders and other people they knew. Despite all the talk about a generation gap, Duane's parents were impressed by how easily his friends accepted them.

Duane continued to help out with other people's trials and support group activities. Peace movement activists were getting arrested right and left, and there were plenty of individual causes to support. Then, of course, there was a war still going on and growing numbers of antiwar demonstrations to attend.

Never for one minute did he think of recanting. But the

point of his draft resistance did haunt him. Was his purpose to
make a big scene? Or was it to remain personally pure, un-
tainted by the war system? How much punishment should he
try to avoid? He knew he did not want to personally be part of
the conscription process. He also wanted that refusal to be part
of a protest movement that would help stop the war.

One option Duane toyed with was to stand by his earlier
plea of "not guilty" and argue at the trial that Selective
Service had all the information it needed on him—his name,
age, and address—and that it should have gone ahead and
registered him rather than prosecute. But he decided he was
not interested in that. He did not want to have anything to do
with the conscription process, voluntarily or involuntarily.

For a time, too, he thought he might keep his not-guilty
plea in order to get a full-blown jury trial. That way he could use
the trial as a forum to educate the jury and the general public
about the terrible reality of the war. He would invite in antiwar
witnesses who would testify to the brutality of the U.S. war effort. He would call witnesses who would defend his own
character and peaceful intent. He would try to embarrass the
humans in the jury whose duty it was to enforce the law by
showing them what the law really meant in Southeast Asia.

But the attorney he had hired posed some other
viewpoints. A jury never bought the not-guilty argument; it
usually incited them and the judge to be hard-line in their judgment and sentencing. Besides, said the attorney, who had handled dozens of anti-draft cases, the argument that the war
would end once the nation's jails were full was foolish—the
government would simply build more jails. It would be better,
said the attorney, to plead "no contest," thereby increasing the
chances Duane would get a reduced sentence like a relatively

innocuous probationary term. Once free on probation, Duane could go out and resume his antiwar work. He could do more on the streets than in the cells, went the familiar argument.

Duane went back and forth on this for a long time. He did enjoy his work in southern Virginia and really wanted to work there full time. It is what he would probably be doing if there were no war or draft, and if the FBI was not after him. So, if he was rejecting the government's right to tell him to go fight, why should he passively comply with the government's plans to jail him? Why not try to get the government to endorse what he already wanted to do? After much discussion with his friends, Duane decided to change his plea to no contest.

Part of the change came because he finally decided he could not alter the jury's opinions about the war. Also, he felt he might be allowed to serve a probation term with the southern Virginia agency he had worked for earlier. It sounded like the argument he had rejected so intensely for so many months—why don't you serve somebody positively through voluntary service instead of sit and rot in jail? But for him there was a big difference. It would not be the military conscription system telling him to do an alternative service job, it would be a civilian court punishing a lawbreaker. He respected the judicial system. It was not until much later, at a trial in New York, that he realized the courts had their own set of deep problems. There he overheard the judge tell another draft resister that he was not sending him to jail because he came from a fine family, had a good education, and a bright future ahead of him. The same judge later sentenced some blacks, who had committed a few petty offenses, to much harsher punishment.

This evidence of the judicial system's moral bankruptcy did not sink in right away. Duane went ahead and unabashedly solicited letters of character reference to be sent to his judge to show his solid connections. Duane's father Luke was a minister, his uncle James Shank was a bishop, and church leaders like Myron Augsburger, Walt Hackman, Frank Epp, John A. Lapp, and many others wrote the judge attesting to the sincerity of Duane's convictions.

The night before the trial in January 1971, many of Duane's friends traveled to his home to be with him. They sang and celebrated together into the night. About 75 people packed the small courtroom the next day; they came from Harrisonburg, Lancaster, Goshen, and other Mennonite enclaves around the country.

Also in the trial audience was an FBI agent. He wrote in a report to his superiors that the courtroom "was completely filled with Shank's hippie-type individuals who all carried flowers."

Those of Duane's friends who could not get into the courtroom stood outside and leafleted the passersby, singing songs of peace and love. The message they handed out said, "Today, inside the courthouse, our friend is being tried because of his work against the war. Today, what are you doing to stop the war?" Strains of the song "They Will Know We Are Christians by Our Love" floated up and down the corridors of the building as the judge convicted him on a felony charge.

There was really a good feeling in this for Duane—being part of something larger than himself, part of a community of people who cared about each other and picketed together, prayed together, cried together, celebrated together. But despite all of that, it did finally come down to the lone individual, Duane Shank, who was running the risk of being hauled off to jail. Ultimately, he alone had to pay the price, the community could not go to jail with him. This weighed heavily as he waited for the sentencing session to be held in mid-March.

His earlier plea of no contest still worried him. One week after his trial, Duane traveled to Detroit for the trial of a friend of his. Sitting in the audience as his friend called on witness after witness to talk about the horrors of war, Duane kept wondering whether he should have done the same thing at his own trial. It bothered him a great deal.

From Detroit, he went to Ann Arbor, then to Goshen, Lancaster, Harrisonburg, New York City, Washington, D.C., and then Pendle Hill, a Quaker retreat center outside Philadelphia. At every stop he talked with friends about what was the right thing for him to do. All were supportive of what he had done. Since many in the movement had not yet come to trial, they told him, they all needed the benefit of knowing the consequences of different approaches to the courts. His particular focus should be on the judge and not a jury, they said. Let's see what happens if you zero in on that one man, saying, "Here I am. I did what I did. I'll do it again if I must. What are you going to do to me because of it?"

Underneath, however, Duane worried that they were saying this just to make him feel better.

"In public, talking with people," he wrote to himself in his journal during this period, "I always manage to exude a carefree, don't-care manner. But I really think like a quote from one of Dietrich Bonhoeffer's letters where he said, 'I often wonder who I really am. The man who goes on squirming under these ghastly experiences and wretchedness that cries to heaven? Or the man who scourges himself and pretends to others and even to himself that he is placid, cheerful, composed, and in control of himself and allows people to admire him for it. . . . What does one's attitude mean anyway? I know less than ever about myself and am no longer attaching any importance to it.' " Duane went on to write that his persecution was not nearly so drastic as Bonhoeffer's, but his feelings of personal insecurity and inner turmoil were similar.

Prison was something he often thought about. He talked with many people, announcing that he had no fear of jail, that he would not try to avoid it. But although his change of plea to no contest had not guaranteed that he would not be sent to prison, it had significantly lowered the possibility of jail and increased the possibility of probation.

Jail destroyed people, he figured. Some should not, because of their personal makeup, risk damaging themselves; the issue was not worth that much. But on the other hand, one should not let fear control one's life. So he probed the subject, in conversation with others and in deep reflection by himself. He finally decided he was not afraid of it, but it would be best if he did not have to do it.

On the day before his sentencing in March, 1971, he stayed up nearly all night with some friends, seriously discussing how he should respond to the sentence. If it was jail, or a probationary term with an agency other than the one he was already working at in southern Virginia, should he comply?

They talked seriously about him becoming a fugitive. Many people were already doing that; living underground was an effective way to draw people into the antiwar movement. The fugitive had a powerful message: "I am here because I resisted the war. Will you help me, recognizing that in so doing, you are sharing in my jeopardy?" In this way the costs of the war began to be felt at home as well as in Southeast Asia. The war became immediate for people. It was not just on TV anymore; it was in real living color standing in their living room, breathing their air.

Duane's statement to the judge at his sentencing the next day was brief and to the point. He was today choosing life and saying no to death. His attorney added that he thought Duane should not be sent to prison because no amount of "rehabilitation" in prison could make Duane change his mind about the rightness of his "criminal" act.

As it turned out, the judge sentenced him to three years of service with the community organizing group in southern Virginia where he was already working on his own. Duane complied. It would have seemed childish and foolish to him to say, "Well, I had wanted to work there, but now that you say I have to, I won't."

Right after the judge sentenced Duane, a probation officer sat down with him to go over the list of probation restrictions he would have to follow. The officer particularly stressed one ordering Duane to refrain from associating with other known criminals. Duane pointed out that this would be quite difficult because, by the court's definition of criminal, most of his best friends were criminals just like he was. He did not intend to stop associating with them. The officer hastened to say this was not what he meant; he meant *real* criminals.

After the sentencing, a wave of depression hit Duane. He spent a couple of days just sitting around, thinking about what had happened. Pent-up fears of jail unleashed themselves after there was no longer any threat of prison. That bothered him. It had been easy to write nice-sounding letters and make nice-sounding speeches about how prison is not a pleasant place, but sometimes one just has to face it. But now he realized he had repressed a part of him that had really feared jail.

For the first time, he began to think honestly about what jail might have meant, the possible physical and psychological damage he could well have suffered. He felt somewhat guilty because a number of his friends were in prison for doing things similar to what he had done. On the one hand, he felt like he had compromised something by getting off so lightly. On the other hand, he did not feel like he had compromised anything because he had been sentenced to a service assignment he was already feeling led to do.

With his feelings all contradicting themselves in one tense knot, Duane went back down to southern Virginia to work again, this time under probationary sentence.

One of his first contacts with the new restrictions on his life came early when he asked his probation officer for permission to travel to an antiwar demonstration in Washington, D.C. The officer denied his request, saying he had heard some veterans were going to be there and that there could be violence. The rejection seemed to be a bad omen for the future. But a phone call to the officer straightened things out and Duane's case was soon transferred to an officer who was so overworked with other more dangerous criminals that he had little time or interest in keeping tight reins on a harmless draft resister. There were no more problems. Every time Duane wanted to travel outside the eastern half of Virginia, he just called up his probation officer. It was a trivial formality. Monthly reports also had to be filed, just a matter of checking no to a bunch of questions and dropping the form in the mailbox.

There was a federal penitentiary nearby where he was working in Petersburg, Virginia. Oddly enough, two of Duane's friends were imprisoned there on draft-resistance charges during the time he was serving probation. He had his name placed on their visiting lists and went to see them regularly.

The probationary sentence was for three years, and it was shortened by only several months. Duane moved to Washington, D.C., for the final year of his term to take up a job with the National Interreligious Service Board for Conscientious Objectors (NISBCO). He had enjoyed his involvement in southern Virginia; it was a break from all of his earlier antiwar work. But he felt like it was time again to get involved in peace work. NISBCO was working on draft and military issues, and he wanted to get back into that kind of work, as well as to live in Washington, nearer to some of his friends. The NISBCO job was quickly approved by his probation officer.

He stayed on for six years with NISBCO, working toward amnesty for draft violators, to get retroactively legalized what he and thousands of other resisters had done. After having married Ellen Kennel, a friend he had known in high school and college and kept in touch with since, he quit working at NISBCO, painted houses for a year or so, and then worked on the legal defense committee of a young Vietnamese man, David Truong, who was accused of espionage by the U.S. government.

When the drive for a return of the draft began to heat up in 1978-79, Duane accepted the position of national director of the Committee Against Registration and the Draft (CARD), a coalition of peace groups and churches working to resist the reinstatement of military registration and conscription.

The first decade of his adult life seemed oddly circular. Its beginning saw him in long hair and jeans in a courtroom being sentenced for refusing to cooperate with military registration. The end saw him doing grass-roots organizing, occasionally in a coat and tie, writing speeches and developing legislative strategies for use in anti-draft efforts on the United States Senate floor. The scene of the battle had changed. The battle itself, however, was much the same.

The costs of his nonregistration decision did not end up being very harsh. In fact, that decision led to many other decisions that shaped his life in ways he is quite comfortable with today. His earlier resistance primarily had been for personal reasons. Now, his work is devoted to resisting the overall system of economic and political factors that generate the "need" for the U.S. military. What is needed is fundamental social change, he says, and he is committed to this in a much more serious way than ever before.

It still angers Duane that the government forces young men to make such fundamental, life-shaping decisions at the age of 18. It was, and is, appalling. One has to live with his decision for the rest of his life. And he has talked with many veterans who had made choices during the Vietnam War era they later came to regret.

Because of his job with CARD, Duane bumps into numerous people who are considering doing what he decided to do in 1970—not register. In talking with them, he said he has found that the most important and relevant thing about his experience for today is that he was forced to dig real deep to find out what he actually believed and why. It was not just getting the logic of noncooperation down pat. It was rooting that logic in a deep belief that was truly a part of himself in a fundamental way.

Of course, one is never completely sure about one's motives. Even hindsight fails to clear them up. But being serious about what one believes is essential.

Without hesitation, knowing what he knows now, he would do it again.

2.
Taking it to the Church

Doug Baker

Doug Baker lives at Reba Place Fellowship in Evanston, Illinois, and works as a teacher in the fellowship's community day-care center.

I t was early summer, 1969. Doug had been reading *Time* magazine, and his sorrow was deepening because of it.

Each week a whole section of the magazine was devoted to news about the Vietnam War. Doug grieved over these weekly reports—the body count, the gruesome details, the horrible pictures. But what bothered him most was how innocent the victims were—the people of Vietnam—all of them helpless in the face of the destruction of themselves and their land. Doug yearned for a way to do something about the war.

That burden weighed heavily one summer night as he left the house to join his college friends, Jon Lind and Devon Leu. The three of them often gathered at the coffeehouse in Elkhart, Indiana, and usually ended up talking about the war and what, if anything, they could or should do about it.

This particular evening, however, their conversation took a new tack. "What can we do to get the church moving?" Devon asked.

It struck them that this was a crucial issue—getting the Mennonite Church to recognize the activities of draft resisters. If Doug and his friends were going to resist the draft, they needed to know that their church was behind them. Ideas—some crazy, some not so crazy—volleyed back and forth until Jon voiced a thought he had been toying with for several weeks.

"Guy Hershberger stopped me on the sidewalk a while back. He said he had heard a rumor that we were going to the upcoming general Mennonite conference at Turner, Oregon, with a draft resistance proposal."

"Hah, what a laugh—"

"No," Jon interrupted, "Why don't we? I mean we could go out there with some kind of statement about resistance, present it to them, and try to get them to support it."

Doug felt this might be a way to ease some of the pain he felt about the war. The idea was launched.

The three of them spent the month of June laying plans. Labeling themselves the "Mennonite draft resisters," they drafted a statement calling on the Mennonite Church to support resistance as a valid response to military conscription. They decided they would try to present the statement to the delegates at the business session of the Mennonite Church general conference. If they did not receive permission to place it on the official agenda, they figured they would take over the platform and present it anyway.

Doug's parents, Robert and Anna Mae, were aware of his plans. They were a bit anxious, too. What would they tell the church people and neighbors when asked why their long-haired son was consorting with hippies and crashing a church conference? Was Doug going to hurt the family name?

The three resisters, meanwhile, were getting more and more excited. Their strategy sessions grew long and enthusiastic, but some worries started to preoccupy them as well. How would the key persons in the church conference leadership receive them? How likely was it that their statement might be adopted? They compiled a list of church leaders inclined to support or oppose them. Overall, the resisters' chances for success looked very slim.

In a flurry of activity, they wrote to several conference leaders, asking for a pre-conference meeting to discuss their request to put the draft resistance statement on the agenda.

Then, immediately prior to the start of the conference, they received some terrific news. Doug had been asked to be an official delegate to the conference meeting by his local church conference.

Within the group of Mennonite draft resisters, Doug had always been viewed as the one who was the most acceptable to the church people, probably because he espoused traditional Christianity more than the others. This appointment as a delegate clinched it; Doug would be the one to present the statement. The enthusiasm of Jon, Devon, and Doug spread to about a dozen other young Mennonites who decided to join them. The small circle's suspense mounted as they drove, hitchhiked, and bussed to the site of the conference in Turner, Oregon.

When Doug and Jon arrived a few days early to meet with the conference's executive committee, they wondered what to expect. The young resisters' initial nervousness gave way to cautious optimism as they were greeted with openness and acceptance.

No definite agreements were reached, but Doug sensed that the resisters had made a favorable impression. In order to get their proposal accepted, they had to go through several stages during the weeklong conference. After conferring with the executive committee, they had to present it to a larger, general council of conference leaders in a meeting set for Thursday afternoon. John A. Lapp, representing the Peace and Social Concerns Committee, introduced the group, after which Jon Lind read the resisters' statement and proposal. No one among the leaders group expressed outright opposition, but several people voiced their doubts. One leader suggested that the proposals would give the church a negative public image. Another was concerned that Mennonites might not be able to stick by the radical proposal if persecution came.

Finally, Paul Mininger, whom the resisters knew from Goshen College, stood to say that he was sick and tired of quibbling about negativism and fussing about the image of the church. The resisters, struck by how deeply Mininger appeared to feel about the matter, were pleasantly surprised by his support of their proposal. In the end, the general council of leaders decided to put Doug, the resisters' spokesperson, on the Saturday morning agenda of the full conference of all delegates.

That night Devon Leu invited Howard Zehr, one of the conference leaders, to come to the resisters' tent to have devotions with them. Doug was somewhat skeptical about the whole thing; he thought that he and his buddies would have to pretend to be pious. Again, he was pleasantly surprised to find that they could talk naturally with Zehr; they did not have to try to be something they were not.

But on Saturday morning, during the business session, Doug and his friends received a fuller indication of how others at the conference were perceiving the draft resisters. Dressed in their standard attire of blue jeans and work shirts, they were sitting quietly in the large crowd of delegates waiting for the session to begin when an older pastor stopped near their chairs and began to berate them about their clothes, long hair, and their beards. The preacher's harangue was interrupted when one of the "hippies" called out to him, "Hi, uncle." The elderly brother stopped short, looked, and to his dismay saw his nephew in the crowd of rebels he was chastising. It did not change his opinion about the inappropriateness of their appearance, but it did seem to shorten his speech.

The preacher's disapproval heightened Doug's nervousness. The very thought of addressing all those people was bringing on sweaty palms, trembling knees, and a thick tongue. Why had he ever gotten himself into this spot?

As John Lapp presented the report of the Peace and Social Concerns Committee, he explained that in recent months new concerns had come to their attention, requiring an addition to the agenda. Doug deeply appreciated John's beautifully sensitive and supportive introduction.

All of a sudden it was Doug's turn to speak. He walked slowly to the front and up onto the stage. The 500 delegates stretched out like a sea before him. He began to speak. Images of suffering Vietnamese people welled up inside him. He became their voice, telling their horrors. He reminded his listeners of their Anabaptist heritage, mentioning stories found in the *Martyrs Mirror,* the lengthy book that records the suffering of sixteenth-century Mennonite Christians who were persecuted by the state because of their faith. He quoted passages from Amos. Finally, he read the "Mennonite draft resisters" statement and stopped.

Doug walked back to his seat through the fragile silence. He was still trembling minutes after he sank down into the chair.

The moderator rose to the mike and opened the floor to discussion. There was only time for a few comments before lunch; both persons who made remarks supported the resisters' proposal.

Quite a few delegates began to express their doubts after the afternoon session got underway. While no one challenged the central points of the resisters' statement, they did snipe at its edges. The real debate, the guys learned later, took place in the bunkhouse where many of the male delegates were housed.

George R. Brunk, Jr., Virginia Conference churchman and evangelist, seemed to carry the mood of the session when he said he just did not like the wording, and suggested referring the statement back to committee for editing. Doug and the other guys were very skeptical of Brunk's motives, thinking he wanted to amend the statement into triviality in the back room.

Their suspicions grew during the weekend. Sitting at the draft resisters' book stand after the Sunday evening service, Doug was buttonholed for half an hour by a married couple who spilled out their distaste for what they called "hippie" clothing. When they left, four more people were waiting to vocally exercise their support for "God and country" and their dissatisfaction with Doug's appearance.

It soon became clear to the resisters that the way they were dressed was becoming one of the major topics of the Turner conference. People would repeatedly say they were concerned about the "hippie" style of dress because it might hinder the resisters' Christian witness. But it was obvious that people just did not like "hippie" clothing, witness or no witness.

One of the conference leaders, Harold Bauman, happened along later that evening, and helped Doug talk with the delegates crowded around the book stand. After most of the people had left for the night, Bauman confirmed that the draft-resistance proposal was in trouble, mainly because the resisters' clothing had become a problem for many people and because some rumors were circulating about the resisters' personal lifestyles.

Sleep eluded Doug that night as he worried, convinced that the resisters' proposal would be defeated. Lying there, he decided to ask the others in the group to withdraw the resolution if things got too rough the next day.

Doug and the other resisters joined the Peace and Social Concerns Committee at a breakfast meeting on Monday to re-work the proposal. The first suggestion, a response prepared by the committee members, was rejected by the resisters because it did not explicitly state that noncooperation with the draft was a valid option. A working committee, composed of Doug, Harold Bauman, Paul Landis, and George Brunk, was given the task of rewriting the proposal.

A final version was worked out before breakfast was over. George Brunk surprised Doug. Doug had assumed Brunk would attempt to water down the statement. Instead his comments were consistently aimed at making real improvements in the wording of the document. When the statement was acceptable to all four of them, they parted in a spirit of agreement and brotherhood. Doug carried the revised document to Devon, Jon, and the others.

"What do you think?" he asked, after they had finished reading it. Slow smiles answered his question. The committee had actually responded to their request! Now for the full vote by the delegates.

When the proposal came to the floor, John E. Lapp read the edited version as copies were passed out to the delegates. Marcus Lind, bishop in the Pacific Coast Conference, stood to express some of the rumors which had been circulating about the resisters, although he did not directly accuse them. The resisters felt strange, as if they were being tagged with notorious reputations that they would never be able to live down. Another man confessed that he had at first been against the proposal because of the resisters' unkempt appearance, but had changed his opinion after talking with them personally.

George Brunk urged people to look beyond appearance, and indicated that he was prepared to vote for the resistance statement. His speech was viewed by the resisters to be influential because of his reputation as a conservative leader in the church.

The resistance statement carried with only a few dissenting votes. With sadness, Doug noted some of the people who voted no. His friend's uncle who had spoken to them about their attire had not supported the statement. Another hand which had registered a no vote belonged to a Virginia pastor, probably because of what had happened at their campsite the night before.

All of the people in Doug's group, guys and girls, had together used one borrowed tent. On the night before the vote, they had been sitting around a campfire, talking and joking. One guy began a spoof of tent meeting evangelists. "Brothers and sisters," he roared, as the others laughed.

Doug had watched the pastor walk into the light of the campfire. The laughter soon stopped as he spoke, "I heard what you were saying, and I don't think it's right. You shouldn't ridicule someone who is spreading the gospel." He continued his reprimand while the young people sat in embarrassed silence.

Doug sensed the man's hurt. He stood up and went to him, drawing him into the shadows. They talked together for several minutes before each returned to his campsite. Doug was truly sorry that they had offended him. Consistent with his burning desire to help the Vietnamese people, Doug did not want to cause pain to others around him. The next day, watching the preacher cast his dissenting vote, Doug ached. He wished somehow that a deeper reconciliation could have taken place.

A degree of reconciliation did occur with some others. Apparently the officials of the Pacific Coast Conference were very concerned about the conflict, which had publicly surfaced during debate before the resisters' statement was passed, between the resisters and Marcus Lind. They arranged a meeting between the resisters, Lind, Harold Bauman, and George Brunk. The meeting was significant in that the people met and talked honestly despite their bitter differences. Harold Bauman asked the noncooperators to draw up a brief public statement expressing some of their thoughts about the meeting; Marcus Lind would then make a reciprocal public statement. It was obvious that Bauman thought mutual apologies would be in order.

John Conrad worked out a statement with Doug. It was carefully worded so that they apologized for offending people, without being apologetic about their appearance, going on to explain their rationale for dressing as they did. Finally, they thanked the conference for adopting the draft resistance statement.

Tuesday morning the group of noncooperators attended the communion service. Afterward they read their statement. Lind responded, saying that he still found their appearance disgraceful, but also clearing them of the false rumors about their character that had been circulating.

All the doubts which had been pent up were then unleashed as a number of persons rose to fret publicly about liberalized trends in dress, identification with hippies, and other concerns. Doug felt that it was a negative way to end the conference, but hoped that the exchange cleared the air, making it more likely for future dialogue to occur.

I n a report Doug later wrote, he concluded, "If there was a trend in the conference, I would say that it was a movement toward reconciliation through personal encounter and dialogue. At first those we encountered were suspicious of us and our motives (and vice versa). As we talked together we came to see each other as Christian brothers rather than as antagonists."

Doug's reaction to passage of the Turner draft resistance statement was one of jubilation. They had asked the Mennonite Church to support them, and the church, through the

actions of the delegates, had responded beyond his most careful calculations and wildest hopes. There it was, right in black
and white: "We [the Mennonite Church] recognize the validity
of noncooperation as a legitimate witness." Doug returned
home encouraged and enthused by the outpouring of support,
but he was also somewhat puzzled. Many people at the Turner
conference had asked about the resisters' lineage. Too many,
Doug thought. They seemed surprised and perhaps dismayed
to discover that many of the resisters were children of
prominent church leaders, seminary and college professors,
ministers and bishops, writers and editors.

After the Turner conference, Doug considered his own
draft resistance more seriously. Although there was much
about Christianity that he questioned, and although he did not
publicly stress his personal relationship with God, he found
himself totally convinced of at least one thing—the moral and
ethical rightness of pacifism.

He frequently read the biblical passages on peace,
particularly the Sermon on the Mount. War was wrong. Violence was wrong. The prophets of Amos and Hosea voiced a
resounding call for justice. Phrases like, "Let justice roll down
like water," became a liturgy for him. A growing desire to be
true to the teachings of Jesus and the prophets compelled him
to new action. Sometimes Doug himself felt like a prophet
called to speak the unpopular truth in clear and uncompromis-
ing terms.

The raging horror of the Vietnam War continued to fan
an angry compassion within him. He could not shake free of
the terrible stories he kept hearing: the farmer, blown apart
while hoeing his field, his hoe striking a buried mine; the
children, screaming and running from the terror of their burning homes, their village leveled by fire because it was thought to
harbor communist sympathizers; the quiet women, lured into

prostitution by money-laden American soldiers.

Doug's political milieu provided added motivation to resist. He agreed with the student movement that the powerful elite in the United States was the primary perpetrator of evil activity in the world. Involvement with anti-establishment groups and others protesting the Vietnam War shaped his actions. His commitment to pacifism, his political radicalization, and his deepening sense of the pain of war, all united in him and encouraged him to seriously consider a more direct protest against the American military system.

Doug figured the greatest responsibility for the war could be laid at the feet of the United States government. The Selective Service System was an arm of the military, it served the government, and helped to prolong the bloody destruction of Vietnam. Doug strongly believed that the war must be stopped; if necessary, individual Americans had to be willing to throw their bodies in front of the grinding on of the war machine to stop it or slow it down, so that Vietnam could be released from its suffering.

F inally Doug decided he must personally be willing to resist, to refuse to accept any classification by Selective Service, to not cooperate in any way with the military system which was responsible for this evil. If it meant jail, so be it. He was willing to go.

Doug acted on his decision a few months after Turner. Without fanfare, he tore his card in half and mailed it to his draft board with a letter of explanation. His reasoning was simple. The Selective Service System could not be separated from the United States military. He could not morally participate in any aspect of the military.

What followed was a brief period of emotional relief and

the feeling that he had acted rightly. Also following a few weeks later was a letter from his draft board.

Tearing the envelope open, he was surprised to find a new draft card. The enclosed letter indicated that they had simply changed his status from a student deferment to conscientious objector.

Hadn't he been clear, he wondered? Didn't they understand that he was resisting? Bewildered, he tore the new card in half, mailing it and another letter of explanation to the draft board.

They again responded with a new card. He repeated the process several times, with increasing frustration. Each time the draft board replied in the same maddening manner. How could he get through to them?

In a final attempt to make his message unquestionably clear, Doug requested a hearing. A date was set. Determined and anxious, he entered the room where his case was to be heard. Several solemn middle-aged men sat waiting for him. His tension increased as he recognized his old high school principal among the officials.

With considerable effort, Doug plunged into explaining his case, reiterating the points he had made in his letters. He spoke several minutes without interruption, indicating that he would not participate in any part of the military, and that he considered the Selective Service System to be tightly linked with the military. He wanted to make certain that they understood the implications—he was breaking a federal law. He finished and waited nervously as the silence grew long.

Finally one member spoke. He said little, nothing earthshaking, simply thanked Doug for coming and promised that they would take his comments into consideration. Then Doug was dismissed and his hearing was over.

He left feeling confused and frustrated, perhaps because

he had wanted to forcefully push the issue, to confront them and make them react to the illegality of his action, and they had refused to respond. The weeks and months passed, and still he heard nothing.

In the spring of 1970, a new system of selecting draftees went into effect. A lottery determined according to birthdate who would be drafted and who would not. Doug's birthdate was given the number 230, safely above the cutoff point for those who would be drafted. If the draft board had been planning on prosecuting him, they had little reason to do so any longer.

Doug's protest of the war persisted on several levels. The statement adopted by the delegates at Turner had the effect of forcing the larger church to look at resistance. Doug, Devon, and Jon began to be invited into local churches to discuss their positions.

A Mennonite Central Committee consultation on the draft, held in Chicago in late 1969, further demonstrated the church's increasing willingness to deal with the issue of noncooperation. Doug was invited to participate as a panelist. The remaining members of the panel were men who had responded differently to the draft—one a member of the army medical corps, and two who had taken alternative service assignments.

The atmosphere was definitely different from Turner. There Doug and his friends had been in the minority. Their clothes, hair, and speech had made them stand out. At the Chicago meeting, those with blue jeans and beards out-numbered those without. Although the panel was designed to represent diverse responses to the military, it seemed to Doug that the consultation leaders clearly supported noncooperation, perhaps even to the point of suggesting that it was the ideal response.

Involvement in church activities, like the MCC consultation, helped ease Doug's burden about the war. But it was not enough for Doug. The fighting was grinding on and thousands of people, American and Vietnamese, were dying. A country and its people were being destroyed. Gradually Doug felt that stronger protest action was required.

He soon found the opportunity he was searching for. In the middle of a Mennonite student conference held at Laurelville, Pennsylvania, in the spring of 1970, he joined other students in brainstorming about ways to get the attention of the Mennonite Church to focus on the war. Doug felt that Mennonites, especially because of their long history of pacifism, should be radically and adamantly opposed to the war and actively working toward its end.

Together, the students hit upon the idea of a church takeover. Not too long before, a black man named James Foreman had delivered a "Black Manifesto" from a pulpit in a white New York City church, upstaging the planned service of the day. They drew upon his example.

The idea initially struck Doug as being a bit too extreme and disruptive, but he was yearning for some way to jolt the complacent Mennonite Church into action. When doubts overwhelmed him, he would take some comfort in recalling that a revered Anabaptist forefather, George Blaurock, had established the precedent for such activity. If a sermon Blaurock was listening to crucially differed with his theology, he would stand, march to the front of the church, and deliver his own message.

The students picked College Mennonite Church in Goshen for their witness. The weekend following Easter was set as the date; a number of them who attended other colleges would be home in the Goshen-Elkhart area on spring break. They agreed that Doug and four others would speak on the topics of the war, racism, and women's rights.

On the Saturday night before the takeover, they met at the Elkhart coffeehouse to lay their final plans and line up the order of their "service." Quiet speculation about the congregational response filled in some of the evening's discussion. One thing made them particularly uneasy. Atlee Beechy, a Goshen College professor, was scheduled to preach that Sunday—on conflict resolution, of all things. Beechy had been a sympathetic friend to most of them in the past. They agreed to try to meet him before the service began to give him some warning and clearly explain their purpose.

D oug left the coffeehouse that night wondering if he was doing the right thing. Deep in thought, he drove home. The lighted kitchen indicated that someone was still awake. Inside sat his father, drinking a glass of milk. Doug joined him.

"What's up?" his father asked.

"Well," Doug stalled as he poured the milk, then decided to plunge in, "we're planning some action tomorrow at the College Mennonite Church."

"What are you going to do?"

"There are five of us. We're going to arrive at church about a half hour before the service starts. When it's time to start the service, we'll begin. Each of us is going to talk for about five minutes."

His father stayed silent for a while and then said, "Doug, that's not right. That isn't a good thing to do."

Doug listened carefully to his father's protest. Mutual respect had always characterized their relationship. They talked infrequently, but generally shared important things with each other. Doug's father had lived out his pacifism, years before, by resigning from his noncombatant post in the U.S. Navy.

For themselves, Doug's parents were not sure what to think after Turner. Doug and the other resisters had been successful in their attempt to gain church approval. While his parents did not see draft resistance as a necessary act of obedience for a pacifist Christian, they accepted the fact that he believed it to be. Yet why did it have to be their son who felt called to resist, they wondered.

"But Dad," continued Doug, "the church isn't being vocal enough about the war. They aren't leading the fight to stop it, and they should be. The war is so awful."

"You still don't have any business going in there and interrupting their service," replied his father. "It's disruptive, and it will hurt the church."

They talked for a long time that night and Doug understood some of his father's arguments. But *something* had to be done. Besides, the plans were already in motion.

The next morning as they were driving to church, the five young people got an opportunity to speak with Atlee before the service when they saw him walking down the street. They stopped and gave him a ride. After an interval of embarrassed joking, Doug, acting as spokesperson for the group, told him their plans and explained that they had not realized that Atlee was speaking when they had scheduled the takeover. Above all, they wanted Atlee to know that this was not intended as a personal rejection of him or his message.

Atlee was understanding. He suggested that they try to notify the pastor before the service so that their action could be handled as effectively and appropriately as possible. They parted company when they reached the church.

Doug and the others walked directly to the front of the church and sat down. As the congregation drifted in, a few members looked at them curiously, perhaps wondering what five "hippie-types" were doing seated on the platform in their church.

Shortly before the service was scheduled to begin, the pastor approached the platform, introduced himself, shook hands, and took down their names. He then turned to the congregation and introduced the five, indicating that they were a group of Christians who had something to say to the church. He returned to his seat, leaving the service in their hands.

Doug was the first to speak. The familiar nervousness flooded him as he went to the pulpit. He spoke as he had at Turner and Chicago, telling stories of individual suffering and recounting the Christian and Anabaptist heritage of prophetic witness. His plea was urgent and his tone passionate.

Doubts about his message troubled him as he sat down. Had he been clear? Had he been perceived as foolish? His thoughts strayed as the others spoke.

When they had finished, the group waited, wondering what the congregation would do. The congregation responded by inviting the five into individual Sunday school classes. That way, all of them could gain an impression of the congregation's reactions.

Most of the people were dissatisfied with their takeover method. Many people expressed agreement with their message—the Vietnam War was horrible, women and blacks were the victims of discrimination. But to take over a church service, to disrupt the regularly scheduled speaker, that was unacceptable. The intensity of these responses varied from mild disapproval to anger.

Other people indicated their willingness to listen, respectfully trying to understand the perspective of the young people.

Doug remained uncertain as to whether their takeover was right, but it felt good to know that the church was at least willing to listen to his concerns.

Another way Doug protested the war was by helping to publish the Mennonite Draft Resisters newsletter. The project was conceived by Devon, Jon, and Doug, with the hope of providing information and support to the dozens of Mennonite resisters who were scattered around the country. At the time, Doug was studying at Indiana University. Jon and Devon were at Goshen College where the paper was published, so they did the bulk of the work. Doug contributed an occasional article.

Doug also continued his opposition to the war through student groups at the university. In the spring of 1970, his senior year, the United States bombed Cambodia. Doug was furious. Now there were even more innocent victims, this time in a previously uninvolved country. He joined thousands of other students around the country in large, angry antiwar demonstrations.

When the Dow Chemical Corporation job recruiters came to campus, Doug was among a group of about twenty who held an all-night vigil in the army training corps building. Dow Chemical had an intimate connection with the war; chemical warfare was one of the main tactics in the U.S. military's anti-guerrilla strategy. Throughout the night the students contemplated blocking the doors, an act that would likely have led to their arrest. In the morning, before they had reached a decision, someone from the outside lobbed a stink bomb into the building. Although the bomb-throwing was a nasty surprise for those inside, it later had the desired effect. The recruiters held their interviews off campus.

One fantasy followed Doug throughout the year. In his

mind's eye, he saw himself standing in front of a crowd of students on the main mall of the campus. In his right hand, he held an American flag; in his left, that of the North Vietnamese "enemy." Using a cigarette lighter, he burned first the American flag, then the flag of North Vietnam. In a speech that followed, he pointed out that governments, symbolized by the two flags, spawned disunity and violence by their demands for blind loyalty. He ended with a rousing call for the unity of all peoples, the end of all wars. But the fantasy remained only a fantasy.

By late spring, however, he began to grow weary of the student antiwar movement. Doug tried to be a sensitive, caring person with his values rooted in the nonviolent teachings of Jesus. But his associates at the university did not hold to the same belief system that he did, and that became a constant frustration. They might be working for similar goals, but their motivations and methods differed greatly. His fellow protesters seemed to be spurred on by bitterness and anger, willing to adopt any means to achieve their goal of disrupting the system.

A far different feeling emerged as he recalled his interactions with Jon, Devon, and others motivated by similarly based, more religious values. The hours he spent with Jon and Devon had been warm times—a rich friendship had developed as they discussed resistance, their appeal to the Mennonite Church, the strength they drew from their Anabaptist tradition.

A group of Quakers called the Young Friends was another important source of fellowship for Doug. The memory of one meeting of the Young Friends lingered with him. About twenty people had gathered at a Quaker retreat center in eastern Pennsylvania, guitar music and candles mellowing the atmosphere. People took turns sharing their thoughts, some of them talking about deep feelings. A woman spoke painfully of her feelings of personal worthlessness. Doug was one of many who reached out to comfort her, placing his hand on her shoulder. As he did, he felt a spirit of compassion flowing through him, binding him to the crying woman and the loving people who stood beside him. Doug enjoyed the moment as a sweet spirit flooded him, moved on to others, and returned to him.

Then, as the mood changed into a more joyful one, someone began singing and the rest joined in. Laughing and clapping, the song swelled, "I am the Lord of the dance," and they danced, singing and happy.

Doug was searching for more of that kind of warmth and fellowship by the time he graduated in the spring of 1970. At the invitation of a friend, he visited a Christian community in Florida. What he saw generated hope inside him and he stayed. Although the group disbanded a few months after Doug arrived, he was touched in an enduring way by some of the people who had lived there.

Doug was impressed by the faith of one of the couples in the community—Roger and Alice Golden. They were serious about their personal commitment to Christ, but they did not neglect their concern for social justice. The integration of a relationship with God and a demonstration of God's love to the world around them was essential to their Christian experience.

Doug took careful note of their beliefs. Maybe he should take the Bible more seriously, he thought, and he began to read it more often. He wondered about prayer, too; perhaps it had greater meaning than he had realized. Without being able to articulate the how's and why's, he felt for the first time aware of a God who was personally interested in his life.

From then on he cultivated a deepening relationship with God. The desire to try to build a Christian community of similarly minded folk kept him in Florida for several years. But in 1973 he decided to move to an already established religious community and settled in at Reba Place Fellowship in

Evanston, Illinois. At about that time, the draft had ended, and direct involvement by the United States in the Vietnam War was scaled down.

Since then, pacifism has persisted as one of his most essential Christian beliefs. In retrospect, Doug views his resistance to the Selective Service System as a good decision. If confronted with the same choices, he believes that he would probably respond in a similar manner.

His motives and methods, however, would be modified. Previously his actions were grounded on Jesus' teachings, but his motivation had been primarily to do the right thing. Then he wanted to live his life according to the teachings of Jesus, but now he would do it in loving response to a loving God.

His vision has shifted as well. Where he had once sought solutions to social issues through direct political action, he now invests his time and energy in building an alternative order, a community of committed Christians. His hope is that, through their renewed, loving relationships, this group can be a tangible demonstration to the world of the effectiveness and the beauty of Jesus' simple teachings.

3.

The Cup of Noncooperation—An Opportunity for Witness

Dennis Koehn

Dennis Koehn lives in Goshen, Indiana, with his wife, Ann Birky Koehn, and is director of admissions at Goshen College.

W atching Judge Brown watch him, Dennis wondered what the judge was thinking. Judge Brown would soon determine his guilt or innocence in a matter involving Selective Service registration.

If the judge looked at the facts, it would be clear. All males had to register with the Selective Service System within ten days of their eighteenth birthday. Dennis had not registered; so he was guilty. But he did not exactly feel guilty. It was not as simple as that.

In sharp detail, images and dates began to well up in his mind:

January 1969. His seventeenth birthday. Already he was thinking that he might refuse to register the following year.

Fall 1969. He was becoming more involved in peace issues. Activities which had previously filled his life—basketball and tennis teams, class president, church youth group president—became less important. Events like a peace club march from Newton to Wichita, Kansas, and a moratorium day on the war were more exciting. Gradually, he moved away from the typical thoughts and activities of a high-schooler. His reading, especially of J. R. Burkholder's *"Christianity, Conscience, Church and Conscription: Toward an Ethical Analysis of Mennonite Draft Resistance,"* encouraged him in the direction of nonregistration.

Christmas 1969. Driving home from his grandparents' place, he talked it over with his parents, Earl and Louise Koehn. Although they had known he was thinking of resisting, it was the first time they had actually talked together long and hard about it.

Earl and Louise hoped that Dennis would not follow through on his idea of not registering. To them, nonregistration was an unnecessary and irresponsible act. He was calm, but adamant. "I think it is my calling," he argued, "And it is an excellent opportunity to witness to others about peace." Unconvinced they encouraged him to talk to some older, respected leaders in the Newton community—their pastor, Esko Loewen, and the Bethel College dean, Bill Keeney. After Loewen and Keeney agreed to support Dennis, his parents were ready to stand with him, although they still encouraged caution on his part.

January 1970. His eighteenth birthday—the moment of decision. Certain of his desire to resist, but uncertain of the rightness of that action, he plunged into serious prayer and Bible study. One night in late January, he read the Matthew account of Jesus in the garden at Gethsemane where Jesus prayed that the cup might be removed from him. Jesus' agony became painfully vivid to Dennis, as he too prayed from his own garden experience. "God," he asked, "is this what you have for me right now?" As he read and prayed and cried, he knew that, yes, it was for him. From then on, there was no question.

February 1970. On the 21st, he mailed a letter to his draft board. Well written and persuasive, the letter provided an explanation of his rationale for resistance. He built his logic on the assumption that evil exists, and that people have a choice as to how they respond to evil. Quoting some statistics which described the American government's tactics of dealing with evil through brute military force, he outlined his contrasting belief in pacifism as a follower of Jesus.

The military and the Selective Service System were linked, he argued. The conflict between Christian and military values was sharp. "The feeble voice of the Sunday school teacher—'Thou shalt not kill' is drowned out by the sergeant's roaring, 'Thou shalt kill and kill well,' " he wrote.

Henry David Thoreau's essay on civil disobedience was a powerful influence on Dennis and he quoted it several times in declaring his resolve to refuse to cooperate with Selective Service.

"If I were to cooperate with the draft and apply for conscientious objector classification, while at the same time my friends are being turned into killers, I would be the 'agent of injustice to another.' Because of these feelings, I have not registered for the draft and I do not intend to comply with Selective Service law. I realize the consequences of my actions, but I believe that I am right and that I am following God's plan for my life."

After a few more comments about the possibility of prison as a consequence, Dennis concluded his letter: "If prison is what my future holds, then I am ready. 'Happy are those who suffer persecution because they do what God requires: the kingdom of heaven belongs to them.' "

May 1970. English class, the last period of the day, almost always guaranteed to be slow and boring, was interrupted by the appearance of the school guidance counselor. He chatted with the teacher briefly, then called Dennis out of class. As the counselor explained to Dennis that a gentleman was waiting to speak with him, a guy the size of a football player came up to him, stuck out his hand, and said, "I'm Otto Handwerk with the FBI. I'd like to ask you a few questions."

It was a standard interview; Dennis had been expecting it. The agent was checking to make sure that Dennis actually had written the letter and understood the draft law. Dennis openly and cordially answered his questions and the agent soon left.

Fifteen minutes later, when classes were over, it seemed that the whole school knew that the FBI had been there to interview Dennis. Three teachers kept Dennis from his after-school tennis practice so that they could talk with him. All had had close personal contact with him—Phil Scott, his tennis coach; Ken Schlup, his basketball coach; J. R. Fry, his former scoutmaster. All were military veterans. All of them cared about him and were concerned that he might be getting into something that he did not understand. They disagreed with the conscientious objector position, but thought that if he was going to take a CO position, it would be far better for Dennis to take his legal alternative as a Mennonite rather than not register.

Dennis appreciated their open concern. Their questions provided him with the opportunity to be vocal about the peace witness. They did not change his mind, nor he theirs, but Dennis felt good about the conversation.

Soon after people in his church, the Bethel College Church, heard of Dennis's position, a middle-aged member named Willard Unruh approached him. "Dennis, you know that I've been involved in the Upper Room Fellowship program at the state reformatory for several years now," said Willard. "It's a very good way to learn about prisons and prisoners. I think you ought to know more about that stuff since you might be going there yourself. Would you be interested in joining us?" Dennis eagerly agreed.

The FBI visit to his school jolted Dennis's parents. The three of them decided it was time to begin some preparations. They sought advice from H. B. Schmidt, a local Mennonite draft counselor who had dealt with Selective Service officials for many years. Schmidt recommended a visit to his friend, Colonel Junior Elder, the state director of Selective Service. "Colonel Elder is a Christian; he's a deacon in his church. He's always been very understanding and cooperative with Mennonites," Schmidt told them. "I don't agree with your position, Dennis, but if you're going to take it, it wouldn't hurt for you to have some contact with Colonel Elder."

Dennis enjoyed the visit. Colonel Elder was cordial and interested in Dennis's motivation. He disagreed with Dennis, of course, and told him it would be best for him to register as a CO, but he did offer to assist Dennis if needed.

Although the visit did not change anything, Dennis realized again that his resistance would give him the opportunity to talk about his concerns with people with whom he would normally have no contact. It also confirmed in Dennis's mind that there were good and decent people in government positions.

Summer 1970. Dennis worked on a field crew, following the wheat harvest northward through several states. It looked a bit suspicious to the members of the draft board— several resisters had been known to join field crews in order to help them jump the border to Canada. To allay official fears, Dennis sent regular letters during that time to Colonel Elder, following up on his visit. They served to keep him in close and unambiguous communication with the draft board. The letters actually were quite bland. "Dear Colonel Elder: Today we arrived in Dutton, Montana. It looks like the wheat will be ready in a few days. The nights are clear and crisp." Colonel Elder had seemed accessible, and Dennis wanted to maintain a personal relationship with him. He also wanted to reassure the draft board of his intent; he was not running to Canada.

Fall 1970. It happened during his first week of classes as a freshman at Bethel College in Newton, Kansas. The campus was caught up in an air of congeniality that was especially visible among those in the freshman class as they went about excitedly getting to know a new set of friends.

One afternoon Dennis was sitting out on the campus lawn chatting with a friend when he spotted his father waving to him.

He excused himself and walked over. Standing with his father were the FBI agent, Otto Handwerk, and the local sheriff. Dennis cheerfully grabbed Mr. Handwerk's hand, shook it, and said, "Gee, it's good to see you again."

Mr. Handwerk soberly replied, "I'm sorry but I've got bad news for you. I have to arrest you."

"Oh, okay," Dennis said matter-of-factly, and then, remembering his books lying across the lawn with his friend, added, "I'll be back in just a minute. I need to go get my books."

"I'll go with you," was Handwerk's quick reply. Of course, Dennis realized, after you arrest people, you do not let them walk halfway across campus alone.

After Dennis picked up his books, Handwerk asked him to empty his pockets. The FBI agent confiscated a small, seemingly innocuous pocketknife and handcuffed his wrists with a strong nylon band. Dennis spent a few minutes at the local sheriff's department before he was transported to the U.S. marshall's office in Wichita for booking and fingerprinting.

While waiting to be taken in front of the magistrate, Dennis was left alone in a small cell for a short time. He filled the solitude with an inner monologue, telling himself that jail could soon become something more than a temporary experience. It might well be repeated, stretching into months or years. For a moment he was overwhelmed by a sense of what the complete loss of freedom might mean.

After a brief appearance before the magistrate, Dennis was released on an unsecured bond in the custody of his parents. He returned to campus before the end of the supper hour, to the relief of his worrying, wondering friends.

Following his arrest, his parents contacted a Mennonite attorney, Dale Stuckey, for advice. Dale was able to link them up with a middle-aged attorney named Gerrit Wormhoudt, who was intrigued by Dennis's case.

U nder Wormhoudt's direction, Dennis radically shifted his plans for dealing with the court system. He had originally envisioned his case as being one of classical civil disobedience. He had broken the law. He had informed the authorities about what he had done and why. He was ready to throw himself on the mercy of the court and accept the consequences, similar to Thoreau's example of refusing to pay war taxes.

Wormhoudt proposed an alternative. He wanted to use Dennis's trial as a test case model, focusing on the constitutional arguments involving freedom of religion. Was Selective Service registration simply a means to gather information about potential draftees? If so, why was it a felony to not register? Was registration a symbolic act of obedience? If so, was that not a violation of the rights of religious resisters as guaranteed under the religious freedom amendment?

Wormhoudt's reasoning convinced Dennis. He believed that the U.S. judicial system had enough integrity to take Wormhoudt's arguments seriously. In the process, Dennis hoped that his trial would force the government to clarify some things, and that that clarification might be of some value to other young men considering draft resistance.

This was the most difficult decision of Dennis's entire resistance process—to enter a plea of not guilty and to adopt an entirely new posture toward the court. It moved him from, in his terms, "a pure, radical position to a liberal, compromising position." Nonetheless, it felt right to him.

April 15, 1971. Dennis's trial date. Initially he was struck by the majestic setting of the courtroom; it looked like a sanctuary for American civil religion, he thought.

He was very aware of his friends, the hundred or so supporters crowded into the courtroom, who had been of tremendous assistance. A Sunday school class at the Bethel College church had passed a resolution of support. A chili supper, held at the church, and organized by college friends, had raised money to help defray his legal expenses.

The trial began at 10:00 with a few formal remarks. The government then presented its case, calling as its first witness Carrie Weston, the executive secretary for the Newton, Kansas draft board, who testified that Dennis had indeed not registered. Phil Scott, Dennis's teacher and tennis coach, was the government's second witness. After stating that he had enjoyed a "worthwhile, pleasant relationship" with Dennis, he described their conversations about resistance, indicating that Dennis had told him that "he had not registered, nor did he intend to register."

With its first two witnesses, the government seemed to be building a case that Dennis had knowingly and willfully violated the Selective Service law. That argument was further advanced when the government called Dennis's pastor, Esko Loewen, to the stand as a prosecution witness. Esko had been a longtime friend and adviser to Dennis, so it was no surprise when he testified that Dennis refused to register in a premeditated manner.

It was during Wormhoudt's cross-examination of Esko Loewen that Judge Brown began to raise what apparently was a disturbing issue for him. The attorney offered a copy of *The Mennonite,* a magazine of the General Conference Mennonite Church, as an exhibit document to back up Dennis's argument. It carried a resolution passed by the Western District Conference that recognized draft resistance as a valid response for its members.

Judge Brown: Reverend Loewen, is it your contention with respect to Defendant's Exhibit "B" that the church has advocated that the young people refuse to carry out the law of the land and register for the draft as required by law?

Reverend Loewen: It is a possible position, yes.

Judge Brown: Is it then your testimony to this court that it is the church that is responsible for this young man's objections and, therefore, he did not willfully refuse to register?

Reverend Loewen: This is up to the individual.

Judge Brown: The church takes no position with respect to this or do they take a position? I suggest that you think the question through very carefully. I am concerned about it because I have known the Mennonite people for many years. They have many admirable characteristics. My question, though, is related only to this young man. In other words I am asking if this Exhibit goes to the question of whether or not he willfully refused to register. "Willfully" means knowingly, with intent. Is that what this goes to?

Reverend Loewen: This is a possibility.

Judge Brown: Is it your contention that the young man's will to follow the law was overcome by his adherence to a church doctrine which advocated the refusal to comply with the law of the land?

Reverend Loewen: The problem that it speaks to is what loyalties one has and what obligations one has to Christ and if this obligation or this loyalty to Christ would require him to take a position that would call for some action like this, then it is a possibility.

Judge Brown: I must say that it raises very serious questions as to the duty of the United States with respect to people who advocate the destruction of our laws by the refusal to carry them out. I will admit it in evidence. I am highly concerned with it however, but I think it ought to be a part of the record. I think it is one of the things these young people have to live with. I think it is one of the reasons for their attitude in many instances.

The first witness for the defense was Bill Keeney, the academic dean of Bethel College, and Dennis's friend and teacher. Keeney was called to provide a brief sketch of Mennonite history. His clear and simple statement of the long tradition of Mennonite nonresistance began with the early years. As he spoke, he wove into the story the migrations from Prussia and Russia, the persecutions during the Civil War, the beginnings of legal conscientious objection in World War I, and the alternative service provisions passed in the 1940s.

Wormhoudt led Keeney through questioning about the church's peace stance and noncooperation with the draft.

> **Dr. Keeney:** There are several recent statements which speak to noncooperation with the Selective Service Act as a possible position for a Christian to take in obedience as a disciple of Christ.
>
> **Mr. Wormhoudt:** Does the church itself encourage an individual member to take either position?
>
> **Dr. Keeney:** I think that one would say that the church encourages men, first of all, to be obedient in discipleship and then to follow that consequence according to their understanding. They would generally recognize alternative service as the way in which the majority of the young men fulfill their obedience but they would also recognize the validity of noncooperation as an expression of discipleship.
>
> **Judge Brown:** Putting that down in pretty definitive language, Doctor, do you mean to state the church approves and recommends the disobedience to the law of the land with respect to registering for the draft?
>
> **Dr. Keeney:** I think one would, from the church's point—
>
> **Judge Brown:** Just answer my question.
>
> **Dr. Keeney:** Yes sir, it seems to be, to answer it, one has to interpret the doctrine of the church because they do not quite speak to the question in the way in which you put it.
>
> **Judge Brown:** I know. They may not speak to it but you are a student of it. Therefore address my question.
>
> **Dr. Keeney:** Yes sir. The church recommends, first of all, obedience to the authority of Christ and to God. And should this lead the person in his conviction that his obedience requires him to disobey the law, then they would support him in that obedience. They would not recommend disobedience to the law in principle. They recommend, in principle, that where the law is not contrary to obedience to Christ, that one

abide by the authority. They recognize the necessity for law and endorse the general recognition of the authority of the state under the lordship of Christ.

Judge Brown: Then, Doctor, I take it that you are saying that, while they pay lip service to the law, that if any individual thinks that his religious beliefs are contrary to the law, he is free to disregard them. This is particularly true with respect to the draft.

Dr. Keeney: To say that he, just because he himself thinks it, is then free to disobey the law would be an inaccurate rendering of their position. They would say that only after careful testing and consideration does obedience to God require him to disobey the state; then he should do so but with recognition that the state may then exercise the consequences of the laws and he should be ready to accept that.

It was a moving moment for Dennis, as well as for the other members of the Bethel College community. Hearing their history so plainly articulated by their dean, and seeing history in the making as another Mennonite obeyed his conscience, gave the supporters a feeling of unity and quiet pride.

Dennis's mother, Louise, was called after Keeney. As well as testifying as a character witness for Dennis, she related a specific conversation that she and her husband had had with their son when he told them he was thinking of not registering. "We started quite a lengthy discussion, why he should and why he shouldn't, and we presented the arguments why he should. He finally said, 'I can register to please you, but I will never be able to live with my conscience. My conscience will always bother me.' And so we decided that he had to make his own choice, and if his conscience would bother him, and he had another calling, that maybe he should go that route. I think he had given it very serious thought.

"I wasn't sure that I would have the courage to go this route," she continued, "and so I said, 'Dennis, I am not sure that I could take all the pressures.' And he said, 'Mother, you will have to get your strength from the same place that Mary, the mother of Jesus, got her strength.' And that is the kind of philosophy that he had."

Dennis then took the stand, testifying that his rationale for draft resistance was drawn from his Mennonite religious beliefs.

The final witness for the defense was Selective Service's Colonel Elder. Wormhoudt was interested in his testimony primarily to prove that the Selective Service System had in their file all the necessary information it needed to register Dennis.

In his summation, Wormhoudt argued that for conviction on a felony charge, the government must prove that the accused acted out of vicious, wrongful purpose. "Furthermore, Your Honor ... I think ... the cases are clear that the main purpose of the registration element of the Act is to obtain sufficient information with respect to the person under the obligation to register.

"Again, there is no dispute but what the government has had sufficient information to accomplish the basic purpose of the Act. All that remains to be done is, in effect, a symbolic act, like saluting the flag, I suppose. If we want more than this information, we want formal observable acquiescence in the system. And this boy's religious convictions don't permit him to go that last step, that last symbolic step. . . ."

After citing court cases to buttress his arguments, Wormhoudt quoted a judge from a related case as saying, " 'When the law treats a reasonable, conscientious act as a crime, it subverts its own power. It invites civil disobedience. It impairs the very habits which nourish and preserve the law.'

"Your Honor, I said at the outset that I would not ask for a result in this case which I thought would bend the integrity of our legal system. It seems to me that based on the common law of requirement of a wrongful mind and evil motive, there has been a failure of proof in this case. There hasn't even been any attempt to go to that issue by the government. They have stayed away from it. In effect I think they have conceded it.

"But on the other hand, when we take into account the real purpose which this law is intended to accomplish, which is to get information on young men of military age for the purpose of intending to classify for future purposes, then it seems to me again that the essence, the substance of the law, has been complied with.

"I know this is a difficult decision. People who take the position that these people take are hard to comprehend to a majority of our population, to those of us who usually willingly volunteer to fight in our armed forces when occasion demands, but it seems to me that in our tradition we can make an accommodation with these people because I think in balance they belong here and there is no other place for them to go."

Wormhoudt's rhetorical sympathy for Mennonites warmed up as he concluded. "They have wandered over the face of the earth. I don't believe we should expel them from this country for a belief which is genuinely and sincerely held. This is not a thing which has been generated or manufactured by present circumstances. It has its roots in history. It is not a matter of vogue or of current political sentiment. It runs much stronger and deeper than that."

Dennis, his lawyer, parents, and friends waited for the verdict. Would Judge Brown find him guilty?

Judge Brown first addressed two questions: Did Dennis fail to perform a duty required of him under the law? Did Dennis do so willfully and knowingly? Affirmative on both counts, was the judge's analysis. He then dismissed Wormhoudt's argument that the draft board had sufficient information to register Dennis by citing several court cases which had ruled that this argument was not valid. But the issue of criminal intent was more troublesome for the judge.

"There can be no question ... that it is necessary to prove culpable criminal intent as an essential element of a crime under this section," Judge Brown stated. "And the problem that counsel has presented to the court, and one which I cannot avoid is, 'Can a person do something in the name of religion and still have criminal intent?'

"While I admire the industry, the friendliness of this religious sect, and while I have heard of the statements of the church with respect to it, this does not relieve the individual of his responsibility. If things of this kind can be done in the name of religion, what other deprivations to our society can be done in the name of religion?" His voice got louder. "The religions of the world which are protected in this country, the rights to religious beliefs which are protected in this country, do not permit the violation of our rules of society adopted by the duly constituted and elected people, the Congress of the United States. When people seek to avoid that, as this young man has done, and seek to avoid it with a purpose, willfully avoiding it in the name of religion, to me he does a grave disservice to himself, to his friends, and to even the people who will suffer the most because of his conceit and righteousness, his own people.

"It is a tragedy to me that this thing has to come up. I have no other alternative than what I have done today. And I find the defendant guilty as charged."

The judge's remarks had been leading up to that verdict, but it still stunned Dennis. Although the sentence was yet to be determined and he could still decide to pursue the possibility of an appeal, he was now one very big step closer to prison.

The judge granted Dennis permission to remain free on bail, and added a few concluding remarks. "These protections which are given to people, the right to be free in society for a time pending the sentencing under bail, all of these are rights which were obtained by Americans who bled and died to protect those rights and they didn't claim that they owed no duty to the laws of society or to this nation. And because of it people can sleep well tonight. But let them look to the cemetery, let them look to the people who fought and died so that they might have support of their religious beliefs, with the only requirement being to register, disclose those religious beliefs, and seek to have them protected." The judge paused for a long silence and then quietly said, "My silence for a few moments has only been because I pray my ruling may be right."

Dennis's friends responded in a variety of ways to the verdict. Wormhoudt urged an appeal. Earl and Louise were sad and worried, but were resigned to whatever consequences were in store for their son. Dennis himself felt in limbo. When things like the sentencing were up in the air, it was hard to know how to respond.

He was sentenced on June 14. Again his friends turned out to support him. Mr. Wormhoudt urged the judge to consider that the standard purposes of deterrence and retribution did not apply, nor could the principle of example to others be successfully employed.

Judge Brown rambled through factors that he had to consider in sentencing: the nature and circumstances of the crime, the convicted's attitude toward society, his mental and emotional makeup. Depending on one's perspective, some of the judge's remarks were either witty or sarcastic. At one point he digressed to compare Dennis to a mule that regularly walked into a wall "because he didn't give a damn." Reading from an FBI report, he said, "Physically, you are a 19-year-old white offender, six feet two inches tall, 155 pounds, and possess a slender build, blond hair, blue eyes," and then remarked, "You would be known to be kind of a dish to the girls."

Several times he indicated that Dennis did not properly appreciate or care for society nor for the privileges he had received as a result of being a citizen of America. When given the opportunity, Dennis replied, "You seem to perceive that I don't wish to be a constructive influence in society. I see myself as wanting to do what I think is best for society."

Gaining confidence, Dennis went on: "I know that I personally am not always capable of making the correct decision and that is why I rely very often on friends, acquaintances in the community, people in my church, and in this way I have felt much more confident in how I view society and what I feel is best for society."

Judge Brown jumped on his comment about people in the church. "Are you saying that your church told you to violate the law?"

Dennis replied, "I think that was made clear in the trial, in that—"

"I don't think it was," retorted the judge. "I thought they did a great job of avoiding a direct answer. I am just asking you a direct question. In your view, did your church advocate the disregard of the law?"

"Absolutely not."

"Just somewhat?" Judge Brown prompted.

"That is correct," Dennis answered.

Shortly after, Judge Brown sentenced him to prison for an indefinite length of time but not to exceed six years, under the Federal Youth Corrections Act. Under this law, Dennis's length of sentence would be determined by his behavior in prison.

Judge Brown's final words revealed what may have been his ambivalence over Dennis's crime. "Young man," he said, "you are a tragedy of our time, or maybe you are a light in the darkness for some."

Dennis felt an inner calmness during the sentencing. Maybe it was because he still had the opportunity for appeal, so incarceration was not immediate. But he did feel God's presence and knew that he had nothing to fear. In his own way Judge Brown had been human and had given Dennis's case serious, careful attention. At the trial Dennis had been able to witness for peace, which was his primary reason for resisting in the first place. Now the consequences for his actions were in other people's hands. God would be with him no matter what happened.

Discussions with his lawyer led Dennis to seek an appeal. His mother especially supported this decision. At the very least, she hoped that the time delay involved in the appeal would give him another year of maturity before prison. While he waited for the appeals process to unravel, Dennis directed his energy at understanding more about prison life. If jail was to be the final outcome of his case, then he wanted to be well prepared for it. He continued to visit at the nearby reformatory and volunteer at a local drug counseling center to acquaint himself with the drug culture that seemed so widespread in the prisons.

During the summer of 1971, he traveled with a Mennonite Central Committee peace team throughout several states; it gave him a host of opportunities to talk with church groups about his draft resistance.

In September, when he returned to college, he used his course work to explore abstract ideas that for him now had enormous practical consequences. In a class with Bill Keeney, he researched justice and punishment. A peace research course provided him with a chance to develop his thoughts about war and peace in a more systematic manner.

The appeals court did not meet until March 1972, giving Dennis time to nearly complete his second year of under-graduate studies. The appeals court judges upheld the guilty conviction, drawing on a number of legal cases that refuted the arguments of Dennis's lawyer. Dennis was ordered to turn himself in to the U.S. marshall's office in Wichita on May 11.

He believed he was as ready as he could be. He had pre-pared, studied, and primed himself for the possibility of prison. It had been 2½ years in coming, from January 1970 to May 1972.

Dennis invited some friends to join him when he turned himself in. Planning a short service outside the federal building, he printed up a brief statement and a few songs, and en-couraged people to bring a flower. At the conclusion of the service, he wanted everyone to join their flowers into a bouquet to symbolize the group participation that he had felt in his resistance.

Driving to Wichita with his parents, he began to feel bur-dened by the image of jail at the end of the trip. It was as if the family was beginning a journey together which he would have to continue on alone.

By the time they arrived at the federal building, Dennis felt anxious and restless. He also needed to use the restroom, so he started into the building to find one. Guards, stationed at each door because of an ongoing major murder trial, asked his name before allowing him to enter.

"We're expecting you," one guard replied.

"All I want to do is to come in and use the bathroom," Dennis said.

"Okay, we'll accompany you."

When Dennis was ready to return to the front steps, a guard stopped him, saying, "You're expected at the marshall's office."

"But I just want to go out and say good-bye to my friends."

"That's not possible. You must come with us."

Dennis pleaded with them for a short time, but to no avail. Looking at the two dozen or so unfamiliar people carrying flowers outside, the guards were not sure what to expect and were not going to take any risks. Dennis sensed that resisting them would be in vain.

His parents were allowed to accompany him until he was booked in. Not knowing what to say, they stood together, hugged each other, and cried. Although he had prepared himself as completely as he could, he was still sad, heavily burdened by the weight of his sentence.

After their good-byes, his parents returned to the outside steps where they joined the service Dennis had planned.

In that brief episode of entering prison, Dennis and his parents glimpsed a foreshadowing of their lives for the next eighteen months. Beginning that day his parents took on the role of mediators and communicators between him and the church and college communities.

As his folks were led away, Dennis immediately perceived his loss of freedom. He could have resisted being prevented from returning outside to his friends. But if he resisted that kind of power and authority in prison from day one on, he likely would have a difficult time for the remainder of his term. He decided to simply accept the reality that he was no longer free, that other people would from now on determine his movements.

Following the booking, all the while handcuffed and hold-ing his flower, Dennis was transported to the county jail. While waiting in a holding cell, Dennis encountered his first fellow inmate. Still feeling somewhat teary-eyed, Dennis offered him his flower with a smile.

The inmate's response was delightful. His face brightened as he reached for the flower. "Hey, man, that is really beautiful. Far out! Thanks." That helped Dennis. He felt reassured that he could make it.

His stay in the county jail lasted twelve days. The days were long and uncluttered, gradually relaxing him as the hectic schedule of college began to fade from mind. He read a few books, chatted with some of the inmates, played chess with carved soap figures, and watched TV. One guy recognized him from the times he had visited with the Upper Room Fellowship at the reformatory.

The jail was located beside a city park. Dennis's cell on the sixth floor looked out over the green spaces. With the window open a crack, he could feel the May breeze warming the earth and catch a glimpse of the return of life to the trees and grounds. Again he felt reassured; he would survive.

Dennis did survive. Prison for him was on the whole a surprisingly positive experience. Part of it was the prison where he served his time. The Federal Youth Center in Denver, Colo-rado, was a modern institution that operated more on a philosophy of rehabilitation than on making the inmates pay back a debt to society. In this prison, Dennis knew he had more opportunity and flexibility than he would have had in most.

Part of it too was his attempt to seek out the good in people and circumstances. Throughout his resistance process, he found good, trustworthy people that he could like and respect. In addition, the sociologist in him was interested in the prison system; his personal experience allowed close-up study.

With some careful planning he was able to break the routine of prison life with various activities, like taking correspondence courses from Bethel College.

His relationships with other inmates were generally good. However, one prisoner named Robert took a dislike to Dennis from the start. His teasing and harassing continued for quite a while. Finally one day a few of Dennis's toilet articles disappeared; he was sure that Robert was the new owner.

Small things were important in prison and Dennis was upset. He approached Robert. "Since you have some of my things, why don't you take everything?"

Robert reacted. "Do you want to fight about it?"

"No, man, I don't want to fight you." Dennis was quick to back off. "Keep it."

Robert did not have too much more to say, he just growled and stomped off. But Dennis sought him out repeatedly for friendly chitchat, and occasionally did a favor for him. Gradually, Robert softened. When he was transferred to another prison, he asked Dennis for some shampoo to take with him. Dennis gave him some and Robert later returned to say that Dennis was one of the few friends he had ever had.

Harry was another of Dennis's friends, a young native American Indian who told outlandish stories and always brimmed over with a joyful outlook on life. Dennis did things for him like write letters home; Harry gave Dennis friendship, conversation, and a sense that he was helping someone who appreciated it.

Being needed was important to Dennis. Many people asked Dennis before he went to prison, "Don't you think it would be more worthwhile if you could serve people in voluntary service?" He consistently answered that VS was a good opportunity for some people, but he felt called to resist the draft. Until he got to prison, he had always wondered whether they were right. It soon became very clear to him that he could do a lot more service in prison than could a VSer. Talk about opportunities! He was with all these needy people 24 hours a day! The confines of his prison were never so stringent that he could not befriend and help others.

The draft resisters in his prison formed another circle of friends. Their reasons for resistance varied greatly. Pete had been convicted of conspiring to destroy draft files. Bill had unsuccessfully attempted to bribe a psychologist to write up a report that he was mentally incompetent to serve. John, a sixteen-year-old, had burned down an army recruitment building. Don, a rather mystical person who used drugs almost as a sacrament, had influenced his judge into decreeing him incompetent to stand trial; he was in prison to be stabilized. Dave was a Christian with convictions similar to Dennis's; he had refused induction into the military.

Dennis met weekly with the resisters and a number of individuals from the outside. Their conversations focused on the Vietnam War and on how things were going in Washington, D.C., and around the country with antiwar politics.

Dennis also developed interesting relationships with the prison staff. One of his work details involved clerical responsibilities in the chief correctional supervisor's office. A staffer who worked there, Joe, was a Vietnam veteran who had lost part of his leg during a mine explosion. They shared many long discussions on Vietnam, each eager to talk about his views and open to hearing the other's. Because Joe had assumed an intense and unquestioning patriotism, and had suffered because of it, he seemed to be able to understand Dennis. The similarities struck them deeply; both of them had responded with unselfish motivation, committing their lives and their energy to causes that were larger than themselves.

At Christmas the prison bought cookies, cheese, and candies and individually boxed them to give to each inmate. When Joe handed one to Dennis, he said, "I know how tough it is to be away from family at Christmas." Dennis was certain he saw tears in Joe's eyes.

L etters were another key to his survival in prison. Dennis had written a Christmas letter to his friends outside that his parents reproduced and mailed to about a hundred people. Each day, during mail call, Dennis received five or six cards in response; some of his prison buddies got only a few during the entire season, some of them none.

Dennis's parents traveled from Wichita to Denver to visit him three times in all, spending all of the Saturday and Sunday visiting hours with him. The time was never long enough; conversation centered mostly on Dennis's life inside the prison, his friendships and activities. Once his mother brought his favorite chocolate chip cookies, but he was afraid to eat them because, as he explained to her, "The guards might think there's dope in them."

A string of unexpected coincidences also made his life easier than that of his fellow inmates. Several of Dennis's friends ended up in Denver at the same time he did, some of them in VS, one of them going to school. Visits from them lightened his load. The First Mennonite Church, located in Denver, was another source of fellowship. When Dennis joined the study-release program in January 1973, he walked the fifteen-minute distance from the University of Denver campus to the church to talk with his friends or eat a quiet lunch. He had additional fellowship with the Arvada Mennonite Church, located in a nearby suburb.

But those friendships and experiences did not change the basic fact of his life. He was still in prison, he was still a prisoner, and he still had to deal with the many frustrations of being an inmate.

One hassle was his sentence. As long as he stayed far away from trouble, he was virtually assured of getting out in 18 months. Any misdeeds would result in an extension of his sentence up to six years.

Also there was the pressure of always having his time and activities approved by someone else. Dennis, with his political skills and knowledge that the philosophy of the prison officials was one of rehabilitation, usually couched his requests in their terms. One of the guards remarked to him toward the end of his stay, "Because you say all the right things, there is no way we can deny your requests."

The guards had power, though, and they sometimes got nasty when inmates tried to equalize the power. Dennis once found himself caught in such a situation. He had previously studied two terms at the Denver campus but had not signed up for courses in the fall, believing that his release was imminent. In the meantime, he was given the job of van driver, transporting the inmates to their places of work and study. It was an enviable job since it meant he was free on the streets with wheels.

One Friday evening, as he was anticipating a long-planned weekend at an Arvada church retreat, the guards came to him with bad news. The other van driver had taken off with the van and Dennis was needed to drive as a substitute all weekend. He would have to cancel his retreat, they said.

"No," was Dennis's quick reaction. "I've been looking forward to this weekend for a long time. You have other van
drivers you can use." Dennis decided to protest their order by
refusing to drive the pickup route that afternoon.

The guards were not pleased. But they were stuck. Dennis
was the only driver who knew the Friday afternoon locations of
the inmates scattered around the city. They could penalize him,
yet they could not force him to say where the inmates were.

Grudgingly they gave in to Dennis's demand. He picked
up the other inmates, but was released to go on the weekend
retreat. It did not earn him any favors with the guards, but the
inmates, hearing the story through the prison grapevine,
thought it was great. Dennis had the skills and knowledge to
work with the system for his benefit. Most of the other prisoners
were not as fortunate.

Isolation from women was one of the toughest things
about prison. Dennis, through his correspondence, had more
contact with female friends than most of the inmates, but letter
writing was helpful only to a point. The women who participated in the draft resisters' visiting group were much appreciated; they realized that the men longed for simple contact
and sharing with women.

On the morning of November 20, 1973, Dennis was
released. The prison's policy of handing a prisoner
$50 plus a bus ticket had been altered to give him the cash for
the bus ticket plus the $50. He decided to use it to fly home.

After a good-bye breakfast with his friends at the VS unit
in Denver, he took the first flight and only seat available—first
class—to Wichita. It was an ugly, cloudy day and Dennis was
glad he did not have to face a grueling bus ride.

As the plane climbed to 35,000 feet, he looked out over a

tremendous sight. The clouds were stacked and spread in a spectacular formation of valleys and mountains and cliffs, almost like an aerial view of a Grand Canyon of clouds. The wonder stretched for miles and Dennis was overwhelmed.

"It seems like God's gift to me," he mused, "like Noah and the rainbow." He sensed God speaking to him. "Today, this beautiful panorama is my sign to you that I am with you, that you have been my servant and that you continue to have my blessing." His body was now free from prison, and his spirit was also free.

Two days after he returned home was Thanksgiving Day. He was able to take part in the traditional holiday activities with his Duerksen relatives. What a joy it was to be back in the world of families, kids playing, big meals, and leisurely after-dinner conversations. He was very thankful to have come through prison without any noticeable scars.

After the initial enthusiasm of his release wore off, depression hit. He had spent five years pouring all his energy and time into draft resistance. Now it was over, and he felt aimless, without purpose or identity.

He returned to Bethel College, but late November was a difficult time to fit back into the "outside." His friends, immersed in their lives and schedules, were under pressure to complete their coursework by the end of the term and had little time to be with him. One of his professors hired him as a peace studies assistant. In February, he began taking courses full time.

Summer came, and he began working as a camp counselor. The constant exposure to exuberant kids and lush nature nurtured him back to life, and he felt whole again.

By the spring of 1975, he had finished his BA degree in sociology. A scholarship from the Fund for Theological Education made it possible for him to study one year at Harvard Divinity School. He enjoyed the year so much he decided to continue in that field. Further studies at Harvard, and a spring semester at the Mennonite seminary in Elkhart, qualified him for a Master of Divinity degree. While at Elkhart, he met Ann Birkey. They were married in the summer of 1977.

In 1978, he accepted a position as a management consultant at the Oaklawn Psychiatric Center, a position he continued to hold into the 1980s. Frequently he now finds himself in the ironic position of consulting with criminal justice officials responsible for maintaining the prison system.

He and his wife are members of the Assembly Mennonite Church in Goshen, Indiana. In terms of his personal faith, he feels like he is on the fringes of Mennonite beliefs. "Jesus was very Jewish, very much within his religious tradition, but he was on the boundary. I see myself that way. I have a great deal of interest in other denominations, in interacting with them. I'm also very much interested in dialogue with other religions and traditions. That insures that I'll be on the boundary because it's only from the boundary that you can contact the outside."

The Mennonite Church's emphasis on service and peace-making remains very important to Dennis. In a recent article he identified two agendas for peacemaking in today's world. "One source of war is cultural differences, so Christians need to educate themselves and find ways of valuing other cultures and religious traditions. Second, wars often result from competition for scarce resources. North American Christians must learn to live with less, so that simple living becomes the basis for a peace witness that has integrity."

Dennis's draft resistance had a great influence on him. He went into prison as a naive young Mennonite from a quiet community, and learned to play prison politics, gaining a new understanding of power and its uses. He had previously believed that lying and deception were never justifiable. But in his role as the prison's van driver, he had been caught between two sides. On the one hand was the very powerful federal prison system that could mobilize the courts, the FBI, and all kinds of specialized staff to bring about justice or punishment to offenders. On the other hand were the inmates who had very little power and were frequently doing something that was considered wrong by the authorities.

Dennis was supposed to rat on inmates who were not showing up for school or work, or who were drinking alcohol or smoking dope. But Dennis just didn't think even a shred of justice would be served if he squealed on the other guys. So he had refused to do it.

His prison friends were colorful and bizarre, a refreshing change from his typically more serious and disciplined life. In reflection now, he says he misses his old friends, both because of their uniqueness and because they shared a common prison experience with him. Occasionally he meets up with a prison buddy and they laugh over old times. None of his Mennonite or professional friends can ever understand what it means to have been in prison.

Intrigue, deception, suspense. That is how he describes prison life. But while prison enriched his life in some ways, he knows that his experience was exceptional. Anytime he sees, talks about, or visits a prison, or whenever he hears about an inmate's experience, his initial feeling is one of rage.

"The closer you get to the criminal justice system," he states, "the more it looks like the criminal *injustice* system. The poor, the powerless, the simple, the naive, the uneducated, they do not have a chance. That fact is a tremendously powerful force that motivates me to continue working in the criminal justice area."

His draft resistance of the past offers an ongoing

challenge. "In many ways," he says, "my own past judges me." If one is that committed, and is capable of so radically following one's conscience at such an early age, what does one do for the rest of one's life?

He is still working on that question. As for resisting militarism, his commitment remains as firm as ever. Non-cooperation is still an essential path for him, and one he hopes others will take.

4
Something was Wrong with America

Sam Steiner

Sam Steiner lives in Waterloo, Ontario, with his wife, Sue Clemmer Steiner, and is employed as the librarian and archivist at Conrad Grebel College in Waterloo.

Sam sighed as he switched off the TV. At least that was one thing Chicago offered—more baseball games on the tube than any other place in the world. He paused, watching the pinpoint dot dissolve into blackness. What can I do now? Nothing, he answered himself, nothing.

Turning on the stereo, he heard the music—loud, incessant, pushing images into his brain, smothering other images. The apartment felt small as he sank into the chair. The walls seemed to be moving in on him. What to do, what to do, but sit and wait.

The letters emerged through the fog into consciousness—little letters packed with emotional intensity. F-B-I. The FBI would come soon. Maybe today.

Shaking his head as if to clear it, Sam stood and began pacing around the room. The FBI had been calling his neighbors, teasing him like a cat teases its prey. Months ago he had been determined and ready to go to jail. Now, after months of waiting, he was edgy, paranoid, unsure of when they would strike.

The zoo. Maybe that would be a good distraction. Grabbing the worn beret that completed his all-black outfit, he headed out the door.

At the zoo sounds of life surrounded him. Children talking to animals, hollering for sweets. Animal calls, and souvenir hawkers barking. He wandered among the noises, stopping briefly at a few cages. The gray timber wolf held his attention—powerful muscles tensed, moving always moving, to the far wall of the cage and back again.

Sam had mixed feelings about zoos; the pacing wolf reminded him of those feelings. It was great to see wild creatures up close, but Sam's joy was always tinged with sadness because unnatural limits had been placed on the animals' freedom. He dropped to a bench by the wolf's pen and felt the cool autumn breeze play with his hair.

For Sam Steiner to be sitting on a park bench in a zoo with no activity other than contemplation was the result of a long process. He had grown up in the Ohio town of North Lima—small, Protestant, Republican. His parents, David and Katie Steiner, well, the thought of them brought knots to his stomach.

He always had the same picture of his mother—her petite frame wrapped in an apron, flitting about the kitchen, hands in constant motion. No such image of his father appeared automatically. Maybe that's because his father was so many things, Sam thought: father, minister, bishop. He blinked the thoughts away. His folks did not understand him. As long as he believed there was no God, there would be a huge canyon separating him from them.

To Sam the concept of God was not rational. It seemed to be a myth advanced to cover a host of unexplainable occurrences. A young mother's life is fatally interrupted by a car accident, and her husband is told, "Accept it as the Lord's will." Do scientific discoveries about the world's origins contradict the Bible? Then believe the Bible and ignore science, people said. What really bothered him, though, were the Christian hypocrites sitting smugly aloof in their lily-white neighborhoods and churches. "The Bible says the races aren't supposed to mix," they would protest.

Politics became his religion. The first seeds of this were planted in his mind by a junior high civics teacher when Sam was thirteen, and a history teacher nurtured his interests during public high school. Mountains of reading, including right-wing Senator Barry Goldwater's *Conscience of a Conser-*

vative, shaped his thought.

By the time he was seventeen, Sam considered himself an agnostic, but he was not ready to tell his parents. He also knew that he was not a pacifist, one of the many other things he avoided discussing at home. The way he figured it, America was going to be overrun by the communists unless Americans were willing to fight. Because he was an American, and enjoyed certain freedoms and privileges, he was willing to serve in the military to preserve those values.

He knew that America was not perfect. He had heard the rumblings of upheaval as blacks in the South attempted to reverse centuries of an oppressive social order. Most of his civil rights awareness came from listening to the stories told by his brother Albert, who had joined the marchers and shared jail with them.

Sam knew, too, that there were problems even in complacent North Lima. Maybe it was the influence of his liberal history teacher. Part of it too was hearing Bill Pannell, a black man of God who challenged Sam with his powerful sermons at a national Mennonite youth convention. At any rate, Sam resolved to make local racial discrimination the theme of his salutatorian address to the class of 1964. When the principal tried to block the speech, firmly explaining that commencements were supposed to be "nice" events, Sam's spunky mom came to Sam's defense. She enlisted the aid of Vic Stoltzfus, the young pastor from their home church. Together his mother and minister were a formidable team, and they succeeded in arguing the principal into allowing Sam to deliver his message to the squirming audience.

In the fall of 1964 Sam began studying at Goshen College in Goshen, Indiana. The thought of attending a large university had overwhelmed him, so he had chosen the small Mennonite college despite his contempt for Christianity. His eighteenth birthday, which rolled around a few weeks after classes began, meant he had to register for the draft. At that time the Vietnam War was just beginning to crank up. But the draft had been in effect for years; it was standard procedure for all males to register on their eighteenth birthday.

It was on his birthday that Sam told his parents of his beliefs.

"I'm not a pacifist," he wrote home. "Communism has to be stopped, and I am prepared to serve in the military for that purpose." The point was clear to his parents; Sam was telling them that their God was meaningless. Little of their pain reached him.

Sam's pastor, Vic Stoltzfus, traveled to Goshen to track Sam down and talk with him. "I'm not going to take your name off the membership list even if you want me to," he told Sam. "This isn't an uncommon thing for young people to go through—we'll see how you feel in a few years. In the meantime, I've been wanting to ask you a few questions."

They talked for several hours, Vic always listening patiently to Sam's arguments against faith in God, but always coming back with one more question. Vic was not going to let Sam off easily. At the same time Sam was not interested in Vic's answers. They were too simplistic, he scorned.

Sam turned his attention to political science and history. In March 1965, he participated in a bit of American history himself by joining one of the civil rights movement's largest demonstrations. The march from Selma to Montgomery, led by Dr. Martin Luther King, Jr., and joined by about 50,000 people, was a dramatic moment. For Sam it was a personal introduction to the politics of the left.

For a long time afterward, the very thought of that march brought back vivid images. Tramping through the streets in the searing hot sun. White faces flushed red with hate.

National Guardsmen, standing silent and erect every ten feet, bayonets drawn, protecting him from other Americans outside the schoolground where he was housed.

Inspired by the eloquent King thundering from the portico of the classically beautiful State Capitol, Sam began to wonder about his commitment to militarily defend America. On the ride home, when the car radio crackled with the news that a civil rights demonstrator had been killed, he became convinced. Something was wrong with America, and fighting the communists just was not going to make it right. That was too simple.

Back at Goshen, Sam soon got in contact with a few members of a Chicago-based chapter of the then rather tranquil and theoretical SDS—Students for a Democratic Society. Speaking on the Goshen College campus a few times, the SDSers offered a challenging alternative to the existing system. Sam, along with a few other students, became an SDS member at large.

O ther marches and demonstrations followed. In Washington, New York, and Chicago, Sam walked the streets and listened to speeches and songs and appeals.

As his political consciousness grew, Sam realized that he could not kill anyone. A conscientious-objector exemption was readily available for him if he applied as a Mennonite. But he did not consider himself a Mennonite or a Christian. His personal philosophy of pacifism was drawn from the writings of nonreligious humanists, and he was up front about that in his CO application.

"Life is essentially sacred," he wrote on the form requesting a change in his Selective Service status. "I believe that one human being does not have the right to make permanent judgments about the disposition of someone else's life."

His application was ignored by the draft board. As long as he was a student with a college deferment, they were not going to bother to change his classification.

Goshen College, meanwhile, had its own political struggles, some of which Sam helped to ignite. His belief about the existence of God swung between agnostic and atheist, depending on the month and the mood. Whichever his persuasion, he was adamant about one point—the college should not be allowed to demand his attendance at a worship service. The way he saw it, it was a charade. The college called the service a convocation, required attendance, and tried to persuade students that it was not what it was—forced religion.

One day during his junior year, Sam was sure that he had an airtight case against required attendance when a convocation speaker began to overtly push Christianity. Sam was moved to protest the forced attendance by withholding his attendance cards. To show he was serious about it and not just lazy, he continued to go to chapel. Nevertheless, the administration slapped him with a one-term suspension from school.

When he returned to campus, he decided to be good. Summer school passed without major incident. But suspicions and hard feelings, on both his part and that of the college administrators, continued to grow. His involvement with the radical left and his vocal atheism may have produced fear within the college administration. Because of his previous suspension, Sam viewed the administration as rigidly intolerant.

He started his senior year in the fall of 1967. Early in September, he began talking with a few dorm friends, Tom Harley, Jim Wenger, and Lowell Miller. Long irritated by the policies on campus, they began to brainstorm on ways to needle the college administration. Together they came up with an idea drawn from similar student activities occurring across the country—an underground newspaper.

In preparing the first issue, a close-knit camaraderie developed among them as they wrote and edited articles, jointly making decisions. Their hard work was not in vain; the newspaper created an instant sensation when it hit the campus.

The name of the paper was *Menno-Pause,* and its tone was often insensitive and littered with vulgar words. It ruffled more than a few feathers. The controversy it caused grew to the point that a sympathetic professor had to warn them that they had better quickly establish themselves as serious journalists or they would be in bad trouble with the administration.

In response they published another issue which included a feature article about one of the professors. The students thought the article was essentially positive, that it would be acceptable to the college community. In keeping with their original philosophy, the issue also contained a certain amount of the now obligatory gross language.

This time the administration reacted abruptly. Largely because of the article on the professor, which the administrators considered a personal attack on a member of their faculty, a decision was made to expel the student editors. Sam was surprised by the administration's decision, but he was furious about the manner in which they carried it out.

A college-wide meeting was called to which all faculty and students were invited, except for Sam, Tom, Jim, and Lowell. Immediately before the meeting, the four were called into the dean's office, told they were expelled, and given 24 hours to notify their parents. At the college meeting their expulsion was announced to the entire community, along with the administration's rationale. None of the four expelled students were invited or allowed to respond to the charges or to defend themselves.

Embittered, Sam made plans to go to Chicago. Maybe there he would be able to get away from hypocritical Mennonites. With his college deferment now void, Sam had to tend to his CO application. Rumor had it that working for an institution which employed guys supplied by the Mennonite Church's Voluntary Service or I-W alternative service programs improved one's chances of being treated favorably by a draft board. Acting accordingly, he got a job at a hospital in Evanston, right outside Chicago. He rented an apartment there with Jim Wenger, one of his cohorts from the underground newspaper. Jim had CO status and had elected to take the I-W option, working at the same hospital as Sam.

Sam's appeal for CO status led within a few months to a hearing before his Youngstown, Ohio, draft board. His hearing was abrupt, quick, and cold. He had done his homework. A dozen friends had written letters, affirming the sincerity of his beliefs. But he doubted if the letters were even noticed. Jim Wenger had accompanied him as a witness, but the members of the draft board refused to hear him. They had just one short question for Sam: "Mr. Steiner, you have no formal religion?" He replied, "No, but—" and got no further. The hearing was ended and he was whisked out the door.

The way it looked to Sam, he was refused CO status because not wanting to kill someone for humanitarian reasons was less valid than not wanting to kill someone because your church said you were not supposed to. If you went along with the religious stuff, claimed you were a Mennonite, and came from the right family or church, the draft board would exempt you even if you were not sincere. He had learned this while working at the hospital. Other Mennonites worked there—ones who had received the automatic I-W classification. What bothered him was that they obtained that exemption with little thought or effort, usually by sitting down one evening with their minister or bishop as he helped them fill out their CO forms. One night one of these guys had even argued with him that the United States should bomb North Vietnam! So much for Mennonites and pacifism.

Resistance. Refusing to cooperate with the Selective Service System. That possibility became more attractive to Sam when his appeal was rejected by the draft board. His contacts with resistance people were growing, the Vietnam War was raging hotter and uglier, and his antiwar feelings were becoming stronger.

He talked with friends, weighed the consequences, and decided that he wanted to resist. When he was ordered to report for a physical in early 1968, he returned his draft classification card, telling the draft board that he would not cooperate in any way.

His induction notice arrived a month later. Eagerly, he laid plans to make a personal statement about the war by setting up a small demonstration in front of his draft board. After some persuasion he convinced his older brother, Albert, a Goshen College professor named Dan Leatherman, and a couple of other friends to travel with him to Ohio. Arriving late at night at Sam's home, they quickly dropped off to sleep.

Breakfast smells greeted them when they awoke. Sam took little time to talk with his folks as he gulped down the food at the kitchen table before hurrying downtown.

Sam's small demonstration involved marching and leafleting outside the government buildings where the inductees were being measured, examined, and numbered. He carried a placard which read, "I must resist because I cannot help mankind by destroying it."

A few curious townspeople stopped by to watch, and the local television station interviewed Sam. The FBI was in attendance as well—watching and saying "no comment" to the press. At about ten o'clock, after the other inductees had departed for Cleveland and boot camp, Sam and his supporters ended their demonstration and headed back home. In the silence, Sam thought, there's no turning back now. He felt exhilarated, ready to accept the consequences.

One consequence followed swiftly. In March the personnel manager at the hospital called Sam into his office. After making small talk for a few minutes, the manager said, "Is it true that you have returned your draft card?"

Oh, no, Sam inwardly groaned. This guy had been a career Navyman. "Yes, I did turn my card in," he responded.

"Well, that's quite unfortunate." The ex-Navyman looked grim. "I find it necessary to tell you that I think you're being a bad example to the others working here. You're fired."

Sam had planned to quit in the near future so that he could devote more time to draft counseling with a group called Chicago Area Draft Resisters (CADRE). But this forced his hand.

Anonymous "friends" of resisters began providing him with housing. It was adequate and appreciated, but sometimes it meant he had to live with strange roommates. At different times during the summer, he lived with a homosexual couple, a drug dealer, and a hippie guru and his fifteen-year-old mate. As his finances diminished, Sam gradually sold his possessions to stay alive. He managed to trim his spending to the point that he was living on 18 cents a day.

As the summer stretched on, Sam discovered more and more of what he considered to be the weaknesses of the political scene. The year 1968 was a presidential election year and Chicago was the site of the Democratic Party's national convention. Around the country left-wing leaders, dissatisfied with the presidential candidates, drew up a strategy that threatened to disrupt the convention's proceedings. At CADRE meetings Sam absorbed a heavy diet of their impassioned speeches, calling for the destruction of the establishment and outlining the inevitability of confrontation.

He watched as the tension built up during the week of the convention. Chicago Mayor Daley responded to the demonstrators like a stern, controlling father. His rationale: if they are misbehaving, punish them. Daley refused to issue any permits for them to demonstrate or sleep within the city, and beefed up security by ordering thousands of policemen and National Guardsmen into the area. The young—hippies, yippies, and many other less definable antiwar demonstrators—descended on the city. The war of nerves between the dissidents and the police continued until Thursday night when violence erupted.

Sam was on the streets that night with a friend. He was in the crowd of demonstrators as they made their futile stand in Grant Park; he was with them as they were pushed by the police into a squeezed, contained area in downtown Chicago, and were ordered to disperse. As the demonstrators became panicky and tense, many of them began to shove and yell.

Sam and his friend were fortunate enough to escape as the police rushed the trapped crowd, billy clubs swinging out of control. Hundreds of demonstrators and dozens of journalists were violently and indiscriminately beaten by the police.

Later he heard the battle count: 830 injured, 600 arrested. The news reports carried stories about the cops' outrageous brutality. However, believing that the left had, to a large degree, encouraged the events leading up to the bloody confrontation, Sam felt only a little sympathy for the beaten demonstrators. In reaction to the turmoil during the convention, and as he began to see inconsistency in the movement which had earlier captured his thought and energy, Sam began to rapidly backpeddle away from it.

L acking the moorings of ideology or religious faith, he drifted aimlessly. Day after day crawled by as he waited for the FBI to act, wondering how close they were, imagining they were tapping his phone conversations, monitoring his actions. He had nothing to do but wait. Constant paranoia weighed down heavily on him. Sometimes he visited his brother Albert who lived nearby. Draft counseling took up some additional time. He could always waste away days getting lost in the rock 'n roll music. Sometimes he found himself at the zoo.

The zoo. As the past and present merged, Sam noticed from the horizon-bound sun that time had passed. The caged wolf was not pacing anymore; it lay panting, quiet. Sam stood and began shuffling back to the apartment. Maybe he would get home in time to catch the six o'clock news.

A few of his Goshen friends visited that weekend. In the past year that Sam had lived in Chicago, they had frequently come to see him, their friendship born out of their common involvement with college publications in the past. They were the literary clique. Viewing themselves as liberated, they enjoyed the scandal of weekends in the city, especially since it was known that the guys and girls stayed in the same apartment.

But this latest visit had an additional purpose—to cheer Sam. When they arrived, his quiet, despondent condition indicated that their job would be even more difficult than they had anticipated. Calling a quick conference among themselves, they agreed: they had to convince Sam to flee to Canada. They began on the first night.

"Sam," they argued, "you ought to run to Canada. Going to jail would not be good for you."

Sam stalled. He understood their worries—he had some fears of his own about what prison would do to him. Fleeing to Canada had crossed his mind more than once since the bloody Democratic Convention. But CADRE advocated flooding the jails in the U.S. as the most effective way to gum up the war machinery. Sam was convinced this was right. He also felt running to Canada would be cowardly—not standing firm and true to his beliefs regardless of the consequences. He listened to his friends, but he did not quickly agree with them.

Something else held Sam's attention that weekend. He could not quite put his finger on why, but for some reason he found himself specially attracted to one of his visitors, Sue Clemmer. They had been friends for some time, had even empathized with each other's romantic disappointments. Saturday night the two of them went to a rock concert and afterward talked late into the night.

When Sue and the others left for Goshen, he went with them. Without telling them, he had made up his mind. Filled with doubts about what he was doing, he was nevertheless heading for Canada. It somehow felt like he had to do it.

He made his moves quickly. His professor friend, Dan Leatherman, had relatives who lived in Ontario, Canada. Sam laid plans to head up there. Meanwhile, all of his spare time was spent with Sue. She eased some of his bad feelings about running away to Canada.

On a late October day, Sue, Dan, and Sam set out for the Canadian border. They talked some, but silence filled most of the miles. Sam thought about the past, his resistance, his decision to go to Canada. He felt like heavy doors were closing behind him with a firm thud on a part of his life. What lay ahead on the other side of the doorway?

Sam had acted just in time. Unknown to him, while he had waited out that last week, an indictment was served against him in a federal court in Ohio.

That evening they arrived in Kitchener-Waterloo, twin cities located in southern Ontario. With the help of Dan's relatives and other Mennonites, Sam found a job and temporary housing. All that remained to complete the process was a second border crossing, again going from the United States into Canada—this time to apply for landed immigrant status with the required proof of a Canadian job and residence in his hand.

The next weekend, Sue, accompanying Dan and his family, returned to Canada to pick up Sam. They headed down to the border for the second crossing into Canada from the U.S.

At the border the customs official quickly and courteously processed Sam's papers. Canada's officials were under orders to avoid questioning immigrants to see if they were draft evaders. But after Sam had been duly registered, the official asked, "Are you a draft dodger?"

Somewhat surprised, Sam hesitantly stammered, "Y-Yes." Continuing in a polite manner, the customs official explained about the dangers of returning to visit the U.S., warned Sam not to attempt it, and waved him on his way.

Long days and nights of guilt feelings marked Sam's first months in Canada. No matter how he rationalized, who he talked to, or how much he appreciated the release from the paralyzing paranoia he had struggled with in Chicago, he still felt that running to Canada was wrong. He was a coward.

Sue always tried to make him see it differently. "What would going to jail have done?" she would ask in the letters she wrote between classwork at Goshen. "How would anyone have been helped by your going to prison? And besides, jail would have been devastating for you." Sometimes he could agree with her, and the grayness ebbed. At other times, even she could not take it away.

Sue was important for other reasons as well. She was his main link to Goshen, to his old friends and activities. And Sam was in love with her. He deluged her with letters and Sunday afternoon phone calls. They helped to fill the aching, lonely gaps between her monthly visits.

Sue was less sure of her feelings for him. He seemed to be so dependent on her. Of course he should be, she knew, given the special circumstances of his life as a draft dodger. But how could she know what he would be like in a more usual situation?

Not knowing precisely why, Sam realized that Sue had made a big hit with his folks. Maybe they saw her as a normalizing influence in his life.

David and Katie Steiner still grieved over Sam's lack of Christian faith. But they were relieved that he had gone to Canada—better that than going to jail. They showed their support for his move in their dealings with the FBI men who usually telephoned or visited them once a year.

"Your son is a criminal," said the G-men, dressed in banker's gray and sitting on the edge of the sofa. "If he returns to the United States at any time, you must immediately notify the police or you will be subject to prosecution for aiding and abetting a criminal."

The FBI men were always polite; they often stayed to chat after their standard line had been delivered and Sam's address had been updated. At one point an agent questioned Sam's father: "Mr. Steiner, what would you have done if you were in Sam's shoes?"

A little sadly, David Steiner replied, "If I had been in Sam's shoes, and had tried every legal means available to me to persuade the government that I was a pacifist, and it still wanted me to fight, I'd have done what Sam did—leave the country."

Finding out that his parents backed him helped Sam. They also did not seem to be bugging him quite so much about the religious stuff anymore. Maybe they had finally learned to accept him, he thought.

The concept of God still did not make much sense to him. That aside, however, he found himself relying on and associating with Canadian Mennonites. He accepted their offers of help and occasionally spoke in their Sunday evening church services—Exhibit A, the draft dodger. Only a few times did he encounter any hostility.

Sam cultivated his life as a Canadian. The door to America had closed when he crossed the border. He tried to avoid contact with other draft dodgers because he did not want to be an American in exile; he wanted to carve out a new identity as a Canadian.

By spring Sue decided to join him in his new life. She moved to Canada following her graduation in May and they married in August. Naturally the wedding was somewhat affected by circumstances beyond their control. Families from both sides traveled from the U.S. to Ontario to see them wed. Sam met Sue's parents for the first time the weekend of the wedding. "It must have been difficult for them," he mused later, "seeing their daughter marry a fugitive in a foreign country, and a not too reputable fugitive at that."

Sue began working at a Mennonite-run Provident Book-store nearby, a job she enjoyed. As well as providing her with a base from which to explore Canadian literature, it allowed her to become friends with Christians whom she liked and respected. When she and Sam needed help and support, they found themselves turning to these people.

Sam held a job as a grocery clerk for a year until he began doing computer work for a large insurance company. After he had been in Canada for three years, he decided to finish college. He enrolled at Conrad Grebel College, a Mennonite school associated with the University of Waterloo. It offered courses which enabled him to carry out the suggestion of his brother Albert that Sam study the heritage of their parents.

Courses in Christianity and Mennonite history and thought, taught by articulate professors like Walter Klaassen and Frank Epp, became important milestones in Sam's faith pilgrimage. As far as he was concerned, Sam was for the first time finding Mennonites who were critical thinkers—people who understood his questions. Excited and challenged by the courses, Sam gradually opened himself to the possibility of God's existance.

After completing his BA, Sam entered law school with the aim of becoming a crusading criminal attorney. But soon it became clear to Sam that the competitiveness and the philosophy at his law school that justice is determined by the best lawyer did not fit with his ideals. He dropped out of school in the middle of his second term.

His next job was working half time as archivist in the library at Conrad Grebel College, a job which, after a few years and a stint at library school, developed into a full-time, permanent position.

At the same time, what had been only occasional attendance at Rockway Mennonite Church led to a growing trust between Sue and Sam and the people of the church. Even when voicing their doubts and uncertainties, Sue and Sam found that they could be accepted by others whose faith was grounded in more traditional theology.

One Sunday afternoon Sue wrote to Sam's parents: "At church today, an atheist spoke. When he finished, someone responded, 'Brother, you aren't far from the kingdom.'" As they read the letter, the Steiners hoped that she was writing about Sam.

By the spring of 1975, Sue was ready to join the church. When Sam followed in a few months, he asked to be baptized. Afterward he talked to the congregation explaining his journey.

"I'm not sure I know what God is like," he said, "and I don't understand a lot of things about the historical Jesus. But I have come to a faith that Jesus has a message for me, and I have made a commitment to follow his teachings."

When the congregation was given the opportunity to respond, one woman asked, "Sam, did you really believe there was no God or were you just fooling yourself? Every time you were in trouble, you turned to Mennonites for help, so you couldn't have thought they were too bad." Sam realized that it was true. His parents, later listening to a tape recording of the congregational meeting, praised God.

One concluding event improved Sam's life in Canada. In the fall of 1975, the American Civil Liberties Union (ACLU) indicated its willingness to work with Sam on clearing the charges that he faced in the U.S.

At first he resisted their offer—out of stubbornness, Sue said. In some ways he wanted to be punished for coming to Canada. His punishment was not being able to go home to the U.S. to visit. It helped to ease the guilt he felt for avoiding jail.

Yet Sue was right, he guessed. He was being stubborn and ridiculous. He gave the legal action some serious consideration and finally agreed to work with the ACLU.

Sam had kept good records of his dealings with the draft board, and they proved beneficial. By late November the ACLU had developed a strong argument that Sam's case for conscientious objection on nonreligious grounds had been strong; the Selective Service had been wrong on at least two counts. Responding to the ACLU's recommendation to drop criminal charges against Sam, the government concurred and closed its case on him.

In early December Sam received a letter from the ACLU, giving him the good news and wishing him a pleasant Christmas holiday. It was to be his first visit home in six years. Sue's relatives in eastern Pennsylvania prepared a reception for him. "After all," explained his mother-in-law, "since you've never been here, it would be nice for the folks to meet you."

In Ohio, Sam's parents were jubilant. They too planned a celebration, grateful that their son could return home. In Waterloo, Sam felt relieved and vindicated. He had always believed that his case was good. His seven-year struggle with the American government was over. He had become a Canadian. Each time since, as he has crossed the Peace Bridge that links the U.S. and Canada at Buffalo, New York, he's savored the freedom of having nothing to fear in returning to the country of his birth.

5.
You Can't Always Do What You Want

Ivan Shantz

Ivan Shantz lives near Broadway, Virginia, with his wife, Cathy Fairfield Shantz, and their son. He is employed as a production line worker at Kawneer Corporation in Harrisonburg, Virginia.

I van was really shook this time. It was not a new experience for him. It was the fall of 1969, his sophomore year. He had spent a lot of time in confusion as he saw himself struggling with the meaning of truth, life, and idealism. Now it looked like he had some answers, but they were not easy ones.

He had been on a discussion panel earlier that evening in his home church in Mt. Clinton, Virginia. The topic of the meeting was the Mennonite response to the draft. Ivan was supposed to defend draft resistance.

Draft resistance was something Ivan was personally considering, but by no means was he sure of what he was going to do. He was struggling with whether a God existed, let alone whether that God would want him to resist the draft. But Ivan was willing to play the role for the church panel, partly to clarify his own thoughts, partly to help his congregation better understand draft resisters.

Ivan had given a short presentation, following the other members of the panel—Voluntary Service workers and a guy in I-W or paid alternative service. Because it seemed like the evening was stacked in favor of alternative service, Ivan was careful to outline his arguments in Mennonite terminology. Anyway you looked at it, the congregation had a long way to go if it was going to even respect draft resisters. He hoped that if the members of the congregation heard the arguments in familiar terms, they would be in a better position to respond positively.

Ivan tried to state his case clearly: Christians, when dealing with their participation in violence, draw the line between right and wrong at different points. Some groups freely allow and support military involvement, while Mennonites have traditionally drawn the line between participation and nonparticipation in the military forces. People draw the line at different points, but whatever they decide, they are still Christians.

However, if the Selective Service System was a part of the military, which it was, he asserted, then another line could be drawn between participation and nonparticipation with the Selective Service System. Choosing not to participate with the Selective Service was a Christian response and, more important, one that was consistent with the traditional Mennonite position.

C. K. Lehman, an Eastern Mennonite College (EMC) professor and former pastor of the Mt. Clinton Church, was in the audience. Seeing him, Ivan recalled Lehman's classroom arguments about nonparticipation in the political life of the government, and borrowed from them.

"It's like the non-voting position," he stated. "If you're going to refrain from participation in the government, then you refrain from all participation, whether it's voting or running for office or cooperating with the draft or whatever. Not participating with the military can mean not participating at any level, even registration."

When Ivan finished, the floor was opened for discussion. Because no one else on the panel seemed to have said anything novel or disturbing, all the questions and remarks were directed to Ivan.

Ivan felt he was pushed really hard. Some people, like his pastor Sam Miller and C. K. Lehman, challenged him on an intellectual level, responding to his reasoning and argument. Other people were more clearly hostile to the idea of resistance and responded emotionally. One person railed on and on, saying, "Look at everything this country has given to us, freedom of speech, freedom of religion, all these wonderful freedoms. We don't have to go to war, so why are you attacking the government?"

Ivan felt squeezed into a bind. He had some friends sitting

in the audience, one of whom had already chosen to resist, and he felt that he owed it to them, as well as to the resistance position in principle, to give a thorough, spirited defense. He also deeply wanted to help his church people understand draft resistance. But he had already registered and had not actually yet taken any resistance position, so he was unsure of precisely what to say.

He began to make statements and say things that he previously had not realized he was thinking, much less believing. Under fire he began to see the depth of his pacifist beliefs, how strongly those beliefs were tied to his understanding of God and Christ, and how directly they were drawn from Mennonite thought.

Finally someone cut off the discussion because it was time for everyone to go home. Ivan walked out of the church thinking he had some pretty tough decisions to make.

He decided he had essentially converted himself to Christianity in the process of the panel discussion. He also had convinced himself that the most authentic position for a Mennonite Christian was to resist the draft. And this is what really began to shake him up afterward. Was he really ready for that?

Back on the EMC campus that night, Ivan tried to sleep, but the swirl of intense questions inside his head prevented it. He left his bed and went outside where he walked and walked and walked some more. The hill looming behind the EMC administration building provided a comforting refuge. There, atop its crest, he did some hard thinking. He did not know how he would do it, but he believed he would have to resist. That settled, he walked back to his room and tumbled into a deep sleep.

Sometime the next day, he had no sense of the time, a

knock awakened him. He groggily opened the door to find one of the members of his church, a young man who was active in the congregation, asking if he could talk with Ivan for a bit. The man offered to take him out for breakfast, but all Ivan could think of was crawling back to bed as soon as possible, so he declined, suggesting instead that they stay in his room.

The young man wanted to tell Ivan that a group of people had met together after church the night before to pray for him; they were concerned that Ivan was losing his faith.

Ivan was devastated. Less than twelve hours before, he had made the strongest public confession of faith of his life, stating that he took his faith so seriously that he was ready to break the law through draft resistance. Before that night, Ivan had always thought making a statement of faith was an easy thing to do, the Mennonite tradition was to get saved at twelve or thirteen. But then there he had been, wrestling with his faith in front of the church and toying with the idea of draft resistance and the possibility of serious punishment. And now, after all that, he had a guy sitting in his dorm room, asking him, skeptically, if he had any faith! Ivan did not know what to say. He hemmed and hawed and eventually saw the man out the door.

If Ivan had been more aware of things when the meeting ended the previous night, he would have realized that his pastor, Sam Miller, was offering Ivan support when he had said something like, "I would not be ashamed if a draft resister came from this congregation." If he had known that it was only a small group of people who had met to pray for him, rather than imagining that it was most of the congregation, it would have helped. If he had been aware of the false rumors floating around about his wild behavior, and if he had known that this was why the guy was sitting in his room asking him about his faith, he would have been in a better position to respond. If he had known that several people in the church that night had shifted from hostility towards draft resistance to embracing that position as a valid Mennonite option, he would have felt better. But he did not know these things, and he felt awful.

O ther things added to Ivan's weight. His family life was strained by his father's emphysema. Although it was impossible to predict, it was likely that he would die soon.

Ivan actually did not have much direct contact with his parents, Gordon and Elizabeth Shantz, during this time, although they lived within a half hour's drive of the college. However, each of his parents did share their thoughts with him on draft resistance. His father warned about getting too involved in the mass culture. "In the World War I era, many citizens wanted to have absolutely nothing to do with the war," he said. "Nevertheless, these same people led the effort to send others off to fight in World War II." Although his dad feared that Ivan might get burned if he got too close to similar people, he said he was willing to stand behind Ivan whatever course of action he chose.

It was more difficult for Ivan's mother to offer that support. She felt the burden of providing financially for the family and caring for her invalid husband. She did not need another strain, like Ivan resisting the draft and taking the chance of having to serve a prison term.

Ivan's confusion and uncertainty continued into the spring. Then several things happened that jolted him.

Four students, who were participating in a rally to protest the U.S. bombing of Cambodia, were shot and killed by National Guardsmen at Kent State University in May 1970. Ivan was deeply shocked and hurt by these random killings.

Later that spring a draft lottery was held which gave a numerical listing to all registrants, assigned by birthdate. Those with numbers below 200 had a good chance of being drafted. Those with numbers from 201-365 had little chance. Ivan's number was in the mid-twenties, virtually assuring his being drafted.

For most of the time since the panel discussion on draft resistance, Ivan had stayed away from church and thus felt no support from church members. However, he had wanted to sit down with his bishop to talk about draft resistance; his bishop seemed to want to talk to him about it too. The opportunity came at a church supper one evening. Ivan sensed that his bishop opposed noncooperation. He took the attitude that Ivan's resisting would make it more difficult for those Mennonite guys who cooperated with the draft to get an alternative service exemption from Selective Service.

At one point Ivan thought he might be eligible for Canadian citizenship because his father was Canadian. That had been part of the reason why Ivan had waited until he was nineteen to start worrying about the draft. But because of a technicality in Canadian law, he lost his claim to citizenship.

Emigration to Canada was also a possibility, but then, if his father died, Ivan would not be able to return for the funeral. Rumors were circulating that the FBI was picking up guys at funerals. And although he contemplated going to prison, he did not think he had enough endurance for jail.

His EMC friends encouraged him to resist, but they did not have the means to back him, financially or emotionally. Duane Shank, one of his closest friends, had refused to register when he turned eighteen. Duane's case would soon go to court; he might even be jailed. Ivan yearned to take that kind of radical stance himself, but it seemed beyond his grasp.

He wrote a poem at the time expressing his feelings.

Two small boats

We met
two small boats
going opposite directions
we would have passed
in the middle of the river
barely rippling the silent water
but
there we were
tied to the same pier
moving together
swaying to the rhythmic blue
of the troubled water
then
you cast off upstream
and I glided down
will you remember
at the head of the river
when all the people cheer

I van didn't know what to do about draft resistance. In the uncertainty, his mind began to fog up and his grades suffered.
Jerry Shenk, dean of men at EMC, noticed that Ivan was hurting and convinced him to stop in for a regular chat.

Jerry saw Ivan as a pressured, overwhelmed kid who
desperately needed a break from it all. Jerry suggested to Ivan
that he drop out of school for a while.

"I can't," Ivan said, "I'll be drafted as soon as I quit studying, plus I'll have to start paying back my school loans."

They talked some more, and Jerry understood Ivan's di-
lemma. But he still felt that Ivan needed a change, so he suggested Ivan go to the New York City summer seminar offered

by EMC. It was a work and study program; most of the jobs involved working with inner-city kids. Ivan grasped at the idea like a drowning man. It was his first extended stay outside of Virginia's Shenandoah Valley, and he loved it. He thoroughly enjoyed the kids at the day care center. He also studied a bit and found that he could find pleasure in that too.

By the end of the summer, Ivan had reached a few decisions. He had more than a few good reasons for being in school besides just avoiding the draft. He liked studying and felt he could learn some worthwhile things. By limiting his extracurriculars to one photography course and the peace club activities, he could concentrate on his classwork. He planned to work toward a sociology degree, with the aim .of becoming a social worker. He would worry about the draft after he graduated.

In the long range, he even had a plan for the draft. He was going to resist in a funny way. First, he would send his draft card back indicating that he wanted no part of the organization. Then he would enter Voluntary Service. His message would be, "I've got nothing against service in the church. What I'm protesting is the draft and the military machinery it feeds." He hoped that if he would be arrested from a VS unit, perhaps then the church would be more open to understanding draft resisters.

But first he had to accomplish his immediate goal of getting through college. One thing he badly wanted to achieve that first term of his junior year was straight A's. He started to pull it off; on his mid-terms, he earned all A's except for one high B. He began to question his academic major though. Sociology was an enjoyable intellectual exercise, but he wondered about its practical applications. His photography course was more challenging, and showed more promise. People were recognizing his talents, and encouraging him to pursue photography. He dreamed of getting a college degree in photography, and then using that tool to communicate to others.

Despite these doubts, Ivan continued with his original plan until he was cornered in the snack shop by the student yearbook editor near the end of the term. The editor was desperate. "Ivan" he asked, "will you take over the photography work? We're only five days away from the first deadline, and we don't have any prints."

For some reason, the photographer assigned to the yearbook was not producing. Ivan talked with the yearbook editor and a few other people. Working on the yearbook would give him a chance to hone his photographic skills, and his friends agreed that he should take his photography seriously. His grades might suffer a bit, but it seemed like it would be a worthwhile sacrifice.

Ivan ate, slept, and thought only photography from that point on. In five days he shot and developed enough photos for the first deadline, working three days straight in the darkroom. Somehow he managed to pull passing grades on his finals for the fall term.

But two more photo deadlines came up in the winter term, and he began to feel like he was running on an increasingly fast-moving treadmill. He finished the photography for the yearbook; in fact, he did a great job. The yearbook earned an A+ in national competition.

It also got him into trouble. He had used money from his student loan to buy photographic lenses and equipment to do a quality job. What was worse, he had no grades for the winter term. The last deadline ended a week and a half before finals, and Ivan had not even cracked a book all term.

I van was weary. The day before finals began, he walked into the dean of student's office and said, "I quit."

They talked a bit, the dean trying to persuade him to stay in school. Finally Ivan agreed to at least take his finals. After that, he dropped out of school without any idea of what to do. He was still contemplating draft resistance. But his plan was not as clear as it had been. For one thing, his friend, Duane Shank, had been sentenced to alternative service because he had refused to register. It seemed to Ivan that the church people misunderstood the significance of Duane's action. All they could see was that Duane was doing alternative service now, which was what he would have done if he had registered—so why had he refused to register in the first place?

Ivan feared that his own action of resistance to induction would be viewed the same way. He had hoped that people would be forced to think more seriously if he would be arrested out of a VS unit. But, unless he was sentenced to jail, it seemed likely they would miss the point.

Despite all of these problems, he decided to pursue the VS route. He applied to several of the mission boards, Mennonite Central Committee, Mennonite Board of Missions, Virginia Conference, and the Eastern Mennonite Board.

The replies were depressing. Granted, he was not the church's most attractive applicant; he was still uncertain about some basic Christian beliefs, like the deity of Christ. But it was still discouraging to receive only one offer.

Fortunately that offer sounded good. Jerry Shenk, formerly the dean of men at EMC and now the administrator of the Eastern Mennonite VS office, needed someone to coordinate contracting at a development site in South Carolina. It appealed to Ivan for several reasons, not the least of which was that he would be able to be close to Harrisonburg, an important factor because of his father's failing health.

In August he went to Salunga, Pennsylvania, for a few days of VS orientation. Jerry met him with some bad news. "I'm sorry, but your VS assignment just fell through."

Ivan was crestfallen. Jerry talked to him further, and they agreed that he might as well go through with orientation; Jerry assured him that another suitable VS job would soon appear.

When Ivan returned to Virginia after VS orientation, he was faced with a new problem. Before he had left, he had been working as a construction worker. Now, because of a severe slump in the building business, he could not get hired back on the crew. Other jobs just were not to be found. Every potential employer asked Ivan about his status with the draft board, and no one wanted to hire him when they found out he would likely be leaving in the near future.

Ivan was trapped. He had no work and no money. His parents had cosigned for his school loan and he could not let them be held responsible to pay it. The family was already suffering financially from his father's illness. He had received no more offers from VS.

I n the middle of this mess, Ivan's cousin, Victor Martin, who lived in New York City, called. He was doing I-W or wage-earning alternative service work in the city, and knew of a position that might interest Ivan. The job possibility involved being a projectionist at the New York University Medical School.

Ivan thought he would at least check it out, although he really did not plan to take the job. I-W positions were the lowest of the low as far as he was concerned; I-W was a not-so-noble way of making money while "conscientiously" avoiding military service. It was an alternative service loophole, a regular wage-earning job that involved little if any sacrifice.

The next weekend Ivan went up for an interview. Before he knew it, the personnel officer was asking him if he could start work the following Monday. If he could, the job was his.

Ivan stopped to consider things for just a moment. He was under so much pressure. Sometimes he really wasn't sure he knew right from wrong when it came to draft resistance, and it seemed like even if he did know, no one would understand or care.

He took the job.

Ivan spent two years working in New York City, nursing wounds he had sustained in his battle to resist the draft. He was hurt by his congregation's lack of support, even though he recognized that to a large extent he had alienated himself from them. He was bitter at EMC and the yearbook project, although he knew that he himself was responsible for blowing the whole term by taking pictures for the yearbook.

To try to forget his past and find identity in another source, Ivan began to pour through a voluminous stack of books, learning American history and culture. He also found some comfort in a local bar.

Ivan did make an attempt to form some connections with the local VS unit, but found himself caught in the natural conflict between VS and I-W. Ivan assumed the I-W guys were a little too loose for the VSers, having a little too much fun, doing a little too much carousing. Also, and Ivan was very sensitive on this point, the VSers were doing essentially the same work that he was doing, only they were not being paid. Fellowship with the VSers did not come easily for Ivan.

He was haunted by a fluke event arising out of his attempt to resist the draft. His draft notice came through as expected after he took the job. However, that particular draft order had been made in the spring of 1971 during a three-month block of time when there was no draft law; Congress had allowed it to lapse while they argued over it. Even though there was no draft law in effect, Selective Service had kept on churning out the induction notices. Finally Congress and Selective Service realized that they had been drafting people without any legal authority. The simplest way for the government to deal with the problem was to nullify all those spring of 1971 induction notices. So after having taken the I-W job on the basis that he was drafted, Ivan discovered that he was free.

B ut he was not really free, because he had to start making payments on his school loan. Ivan stayed with the job, and felt miserable. By that point he felt as if he had made a total fool of himself. He had not finished college or entered VS, and now he was stuck at a frustrating, boring job. He figured he had betrayed his friends, his church, and his moral values because he had not resisted.

By October 1973, Ivan was ready to return to Virginia, thinking he would take some classes at EMC and maybe get a degree in English. He studied for a short time, but dropped out as a part-time job at a group home for young boys became more interesting and demanding. Ivan discovered new strengths in himself while encouraging the kids toward more responsible behavior. In late 1975 he married Cathy Fairfield, a woman he had once thought of as being his boyfriend's "kid sister." They've since settled on an old farm with their son in the Shenandoah Valley near Harrisonburg, where they raise and train a few horses, and offer horse-riding lessons. The group home where he worked closed in 1981, and Ivan began working as a laborer at an aluminum plant.

Ivan's pacifism remains a strong belief in his life, even in a world he now sees to be so complex that simple answers are insufficient. He still believes violence is self-defeating, but says he can now understand why people in oppressive situations feel that violence is their only possible response.

Although Ivan really cares about the Mennonite Church, he admits he gets too angry and discouraged to settle into consistent involvement. He believes that the church should struggle to respond to the needs and hurts of society. Instead, he sees the church spending most of its time and resources on enlarging and maintaining its buildings and organizations.

During the 1980 military draft registration, the church Ivan was attending was discussing the story of a young, local Mennonite who was considering not registering. One of the men in the class remarked that this lad was not very Christian in his softball playing because of his swearing and poor sportsmanship. Apparently he thought that the young man could not be a peace-loving Mennonite because he was not peaceful about his softball playing.

Ivan remembers just looking at the accuser, sadly and angrily, and shaking his head. He was too upset to even respond. But he found himself wishing that he could talk to the young resister and offer him a bit of support.

6.
A Time for Nonconformity and Adventure

Jim Hochstedler

Jim Hochstedler lives near Gilman, Wisconsin, with his wife, Elsie Witmer Hochstedler, and their son. They own and operate an 80-acre dairy farm.

J im looked up and saw it coming. It was all over. Three cars, one right after another, were barreling up the little muddy road that wound around and about until it reached the lane into Resurrection City, his latest "underground" home.

It had been quite hot that summer day in Alabama, and he had been building fence for the community as he had done for the last month.

Jim walked slowly, deliberately to the outhouse. He was sure they were coming for him and the john was the nearest thing to a hideout he could find on the spur of the moment.

Sitting in the darkened outhouse, he peered out a crack in the wooden wall. The three cars, doors open, slid to a stop, and seven FBI men came out running. The armed posse nervously had the whole place covered in no time flat; the outhouse was soon surrounded.

T he agents banged on the door of the john asking him who he was, wanting to see some identification. Jim did not have any, and it did not make any difference. They knew who he was, and he knew that they knew he knew. It was all over.

In less than five minutes, they questioned him, put him in cuffs, stuffed him into one of the cars, and sped off to jail. Jim was not even allowed time to go inside to his room to collect any personal items, much less grab a shirt.

"Buddy, you know something?" said one cop after they were underway, "it's been a long time."

That was too true. He had been underground for about six months, and before that, in Canada for about eighteen months. To Jim it felt like decades.

So much had happened, so many insignificant little decisions that had all added up to bring him to this point. He would have hardly dreamed it would turn out this way, but looking back, it was understandable. There were these hundreds of forks in the road, decision points, and there would be many more.

Just a few weeks earlier, there had been a real fork in the road. He had been at Koinonia Farms, a Christian, interracial community in Georgia, and had called home to his parents in Indiana. After he had filled them in on a few of his latest adventures, his mom said, "Well, do you want to go back to Canada?" With little thought, Jim replied that maybe he would if he had a ride back up there.

A loud voice wakened him early the next morning. "Hello, is Jim Hochstedler there? Hello?" Half asleep, he thought it was the police. But it was his parents. They were ready to take him back to Canada, having driven most of the night to get to Georgia.

Jim actually didn't want to go back to Canada. And he was a bit shocked at his parents. Surely their car was marked by the police, and chances were slim that they could get him across the border without them and him getting caught. Besides, it would feel like he was imposing on his parents. They had their life, he had his. Taking care of his life was his own responsibility. They left Georgia together, but instead of heading toward Canada, Jim asked them to take him to Resurrection City, a counter-culture farm community in Alabama. A few times later he wished he had taken the road north at that point, even though he was not one to ever regret past decisions.

Nearly every moment he spent underground as a fugitive, Jim thought could be his last. He knew every cop he saw might be after him. When people called out his real name, his blood ran cold. Trusting people was difficult; who knows who might talk too much or notify the police.

Sometimes events were confounding. Was it mere circumstance or was it planned? Everyone and everything could be cause for suspicion. His freedom was hanging in a very delicate balance. He was a fugitive from the law and it was a laugh to think he would not be punished with a very lengthy jail sentence if caught.

Jim always sensed that the cops were on his trail, but he could never prove it. Once he thought for sure they had caught up with him. He had been down in Florida with a group of people. They left to go north to Philadelphia, but the car was full so they put Jim on a bus. He had no money, just a bus ticket. And his luck ran out.

He had to change buses at two o'clock in the morning in a little place called Valdesta, Georgia. While waiting for the bus, he walked around a bit. Suddenly he was pinned down by the flashlight of a local policeman. The cop wanted to see some identification. Jim had none. So the policeman scolded him and went off, probably to run a check.

Three hours later, right before his bus was due to depart, the same flashlight pinned him down again, this time as he was huddled in the back of an empty bus trying to keep warm and stay out of sight.

The police hauled Jim off to jail, where they put him in the drunk tank. Cockroaches scurried around in his bed every time he moved. Each morning at four o'clock the lights were turned on in his eyes. The cops repeatedly questioned him about what he did and about the people he had been traveling with, presumably on the basis of information they had gotten out of his duffel bag.

None in the group were draft resisters, so Jim readily answered the cops' questions. But he did not tell them he was a draft resister, nor did he give them his real name, even though he was sure later the FBI had put the local cops up to this, try-ing to lead Jim on so that he would let them stumble onto more resisters. After three days they set him free, just at the right time to catch the bus going his way. As he went out the door, Jim clearly heard someone among the guards say his real name.

It was a perfect example of the contradiction of being underground; there was this euphoric sense of absolute freedom, mixed with a never-ending fear that this was his last free moment.

During that half year, Jim sometimes felt like others tried to put him up on their own radical pedestal. People were fas-cinated by his resistance, loved to meet him, talk to him, try to find out what made him tick. But he would find out later some of them were not honest with him, and some thought it was their duty to inform the authorities of his whereabouts. Yet without the help of many, many people who kept mum, Jim would never have been able to survive for any length of time underground.

Resisting hung over everything he did, grinding away on him day and night. Jim was other people's reminder of the con-tinuing carnage in Southeast Asia. When he walked into a room, he would sense that his presence changed the subject of conversation. Everyone wanted to talk with him about the war or the resistance movement. Everyone had an opinion they wanted to share. Jim's act of open resistance made his opinions irretrievably public, allowing him little privacy. He could not forget his resistance status for one minute. He was Jim-the-Resister.

When Jim-the-Resister spoke in churches, he relied heavily on an official statement, adopted at the 1969 Men-nonite Church conference at Turner, Oregon, which supported draft resistance as a valid option for Mennonite COs. Before the Turner conference it had seemed to him that the churches were trying to isolate the young Mennonite antiwar radicals.

The sense of isolation was not new to Jim. He had been something of a loner since childhood. He made only a handful of close friends in school and his older brother Eli was a close friend. The seeds of Jim's individuality were sown young. A neighboring dairy farmer used to tell him about the month he had spent in jail during World War I for refusing to serve in the military. It was scary. The guy said he had been pale, weak, and nearly blind by the time he got out. Yet the image remained in Jim's mind. Jim's thinking was also stirred up by the preacher at their church, Charles Haarer. He would preach challenging sermons, always asking questions that forced people to rethink their ideas.

When Jim began high school, the family moved from southern Indiana to Kokomo. His older brother, Eli, would come home from college and tell exciting stories about being in civil rights marches and getting badly beaten in jail. Jim became a vociferous reader. He was glued to the newspapers, to *Time, Newsweek,* and anything else he could get his hands on. The world was fascinating. From the things he was reading and from his family's influence, he was sure that he was not interested in being involved in the Vietnam War, or any war for that matter.

Being who he was, Jim generally kept his ideas to himself. It was Eli, however, who gradually began to pull them out of Jim during late-night discussions, and influenced him to make his views more public, as a cause.

In April 1967, when he was a high school sophomore, Jim wrote a letter to the editor of the daily *Kokomo Morning Times,* decrying the U.S. fire bombing and killing of civilians in Vietnam and urging that the U.S. pull out. The editor printed it, under an apologetic headline, "He Has the Right to Say It."

The war had fascinated him for quite some time. The previous year, at age 15, Jim had spent three months writing a novel set in a South American country caught in guerrilla warfare. He would think it out in his head while riding on the school bus and put it on paper when he got home. He described the war in repulsive detail. The main character was a hero who does everything right but has everything go wrong for him, like when he mistakenly kills his father who was fighting on the other side. The book ended with the hero being just another dead body on a heap of rubble, having fought since he was a child. Some of the publishing houses Jim sent it to seemed to seriously consider printing it, but no one finally accepted it. It was perhaps too anti-heroic, too depressing.

One set of his writings did get published by *With*, the Mennonite youth magazine. In the summer of 1969, *With* printed some edited letters Jim and Eli had written back and forth to each other during the previous year when Jim's eighteenth birthday was in sight and they were hammering out whether or not he should register for the draft as required by law.

In one of the last letters of the series, Jim made it clear why he had decided not to register. "I cannot cooperate with a system which tells other men that they must kill and be killed," he wrote. "When other men are not affected by my CO stand, it is time to stand against that system which tells other men they must fight." If it was a crime to kill somebody, Jim went on to say, then he was not going to help someone kill. I-W may have been all right when there was not a war, but when there was a war it was kind of a cop-out.

What really hung in the balance for him was the question of exactly how he would resist. He did not want to waste away five years in jail. But he thought he had to do something about the war. He could not see the point of registering if he later planned not to cooperate.

Jim wrote a short note to his draft board in late 1968,

explaining why he was not registering now that he was 18. He hand-delivered it to a clerk at the front desk of the draft board office who was very nervous as she opened and read it in front of him. Later, the draft board sent him a reply which, in so many words, said that surely Jim did not mean what he was saying.

By the end of his senior year in high school, Jim was very open about his beliefs. His inclinations were a scandal to most people around him, except for a few friends, one of whom was a high school math teacher who was something of a radical himself. Jim also got along pretty well with Clayton Sommers, the pastor of the Hochstedler's church, Parkview Mennonite. Clayton asked Jim to get up front one Sunday morning to defend his stance and field questions from the congregation. However, none of the members openly argued with him. They stated their views, he stated his, and that was that.

Jim was viewed by many as being too young for his thoughts. Few people considered him to be old enough to know what he was doing. The way he saw it, however, 18 years old was an awfully late point to get started thinking about war and the draft. Later, he realized that perhaps some of his radicalism was motivated by the desire to prove and assert himself, to give himself some breathing room.

Some of his high school peers tested his conviction. One guy tried to pick a fight with him to see if he would fight back. He heard that some football players planned to ambush him on his way to school one morning, cut off his hair, and smear catsup on his head. He unknowingly foiled their plan when his car broke down and he rode the bus that day.

In April 1969 an FBI agent tracked him down while he was working with his dad insulating a house on a Saturday morning. The agent wanted to make sure Jim knew what he was doing, and politely tried to talk him out of it. He even was carrying a newspaper clipping that announced that Jim had gotten a scholarship to attend Hesston College, a Mennonite junior college in Kansas, the following fall. At the end of their conversation, he asked Jim if he planned to be at home in early June. Jim said he probably would be, and the agent left.

Jim called Hesston College soon afterward, asking if they would accept a draft resister. The people at the other end of the line were flabbergasted. Hesston was not going to recall Jim's acceptance letter or scholarship, they said, but they would not tolerate him going through with this resisting as their student.

L ater, Jim carried what turned out to be his last note into the draft board office. This time the supervising clerk argued with him about his stance for a while and then, in exasperation, said, "Well, why don't you just go to Canada?" It hit him. Was she reading his mind? He had not tried to deceive the FBI guy about his intentions—he honestly did not yet know what he might do. At the same time, if he even so much as hinted that he might run to Canada, he knew he would be picked up in minutes.

Jim had planned all along not to show up for his high school graduation ceremonies. He had told the school that he did not think he should have to go through some meaningless ceremony to get what he had earned through hard work. As it turned out, a more important reason to skip graduation emerged.

He finished his classes that spring and then, very suddenly, a way opened up for him to go to Canada, and he went. He believed that the government may have begun to get an inkling that he might leave for Canada, so he left when he had the opportunity.

Getting to Canada required two trips, one to nail down proof of job and residence and a second to formally immigrate. A friend of Jim's asked his father to drive Jim across the border. His friend's father was sympathetic and agreed to do it. He had a nice car and it was made to look to the border guards like a father-son business trip.

Once in Ontario, Jim took a bus to the Hamilton, Ontario, Voluntary Service unit house where, exhausted by the tension of the trip and decision, he slept for a full day. He got his papers and arrangements in order in a few days and was driven down to the border by Herman Enns, a Canadian Mennonite preacher, for the second and final trip back and forth through the border.

Jim borrowed a suit for the trip and got some advice on how to handle the border questions. All went well until the U.S. guard opened the car trunk and began to poke through Jim's duffel bag. The officer asked Enns whether Jim was a hitchhiker he had picked up. No, he said, I know him. The guard asked this same question two more times. Finally he waved them through—a line of cars had begun to stack up behind them.

Being in Canada was pretty exciting at the outset; it was his first experience living away from home. He let his hair grow longer sometimes, though it was never unusually long for that era. His daily uniform was made up of an army jacket, an army duffel bag, and a guitar slung over his shoulder. And while he kept himself clean, he was not exactly the model of what was then considered clean-cut.

Jim worked during the summers with a church organization, Fraser Lake Camp, in northern Ontario. While there, he met a young Canadian, Elsie Witmer, whom he later married.

Her church youth group came to camp to help clean it for the summer program and she was supposed to contact Jim to get his help in preparing for a meeting on draft resistance in Waterloo. They began to see each other irregularly.

Between camp work that year, Jim tried to bring in a few dollars with his guitar at coffeehouses, singing and playing folk music he had written. After about a year, he enrolled in what was the equivalent of his first year in college in Ontario, grade 13. However, his attention was gradually diverted from schoolwork by his involvement with an underground student newspaper called *Deviation*. Studies, except for history, began to get less and less of his time.

At first Jim was something of a curiosity. Many of the Canadian church leaders wanted to talk to him. He was doing radical things and they were fascinated by what motivated him.

Canadian Mennonites were generally accepting of young draft resisters like Jim. The churches there have a history of fleeing from compulsory military service, and many people still remember what it meant to dodge a military draft. Jim became involved on his own, as well as with the Mennonite churches, in counseling Americans who, like himself, had come across the border to escape the draft.

However, over the course of the 18 months he spent in Canada, Jim gradually began to resent the way some Canadian Mennonite church leaders were acting. He believed that useful "draft dodger" programs were being neglected and that important ideas were being ignored.

When an invitation arrived in late 1970 for him to return to the U.S. to speak at a conference on "alternative lifestyles" at the Mennonite seminary in Elkhart, Indiana, he jumped at the chance. Being a fugitive from the law, he knew that he would make quite a splash there. The trip would put some pizzazz back into his life.

He hitchhiked into Kitchener, Ontario, on a bitterly cold morning to catch a ride down to the Elkhart conference with some Canadian seminary students. Returning to the U.S. was risky business. But there were no problems at the border this time; for official purposes, he was just one of the seminary students going to a meeting in Indiana.

The conference was worth the trip. He felt as if he was an important part of the antiwar movement again. There was no longer any question of his sincerity. People paid attention to him because he was putting his life on the line. Jim was surprised to meet his brother at the conference. Talking it over with Eli, Jim decided to stay underground in the U.S.

After the conference, Jim and Eli drove down to their parents' home outside of Kokomo, just two hours south of Elkhart. Jim's mother was making supper, putting together a lemon pie, when Jim walked in the door. Jim! She could not believe it. He was supposed to be in Canada, safe and secure from the government's punishment. It was so dangerous, no one must know about this. She could not understand why he was taking such a risk. Thoughts aswirl, she kept on making supper.

When they were ready for dessert, she pulled the lemon pie off the kitchen counter and let Jim cut the first piece. He took one bite and came up with a puzzled look. "Mom! What's wrong with this thing?" In all her fear and excitement, she had forgotten to bake the pie!

Mary and Milo Hochstedler had been lonely ever since Jim had gone to Canada. People at their church, Parkview Mennonite, just did not talk to them about Jim's draft resistance. Still, the Hochstedlers figured a good deal was being said behind their backs. Those who did talk to them face-to-face about Jim went on at length about how he was threatening the church's alternative service by his resistance, and worried about how Jim's action might adversely affect the rest of them. Mary especially felt the disapproval. She wanted to be accepted by people, and took what they said personally. A friend of Mary's even refused to talk to her for a while after she and Milo helped Jim get to Canada. Mary's friends could not believe she was helping a lawbreaker, even if he was her own son.

Jim knew it was hard for his parents, but he did not really talk it over much with them. They knew what his convictions were. Even though they disagreed with what he did, they just figured that he had to do what he felt he had to do. There were many things he did not discuss with them, but he was still their son. Nothing could change that.

Mary and Milo had gone up to Canada to see Jim twice while he was there. They had a friend with relatives in Kitchener-Waterloo who opened their home to the Hochstedlers when they came to visit.

But when they got back home from their visits with Jim, Mary and Milo just tried to forget the whole thing most of the time. And although the neighbors appeared to not be able to accept young radicals like Jim, they seemed to forget about him while he was in Canada.

Jim's return to the U.S. upset the community again. An FBI agent began to make regular visits out to the Hochstedler farm, always managing to come when Milo was away and Mary was home alone. The FBI man would be most polite, but persistently asked Mary for Jim's address and whereabouts. He was frank about it, trying to convince Mary that it would be the best thing for Jim to be apprehended and jailed. Mary was tempted sometimes by his nice, smooth arguments, but she knew that she could never give in. She was not a turncoat parent. Nor was Milo. He said more than once that if the FBI guy came around when he was home, he would tell him to leave. Milo suspected that the government was even tapping their phones, trying to catch Jim when he called.

One day while the FBI guy was quizzing Mary in the living room, the phone rang and she got up and went to another room to answer it. When she came back, the FBI guy was still sitting where she had left him.

A few weeks later, the FBI arrested Jim in Alabama. An idea hit her. There had been a letter from Jim sitting in a little stack of mail by the living-room door the last time the FBI had visited. It did not have his name on it, just an anonymous return address. That must have been one of the ways the government had tracked Jim down, sneaking through their mail while she was on the phone.

Mary never heard from the FBI agent again. He lived in nearby Kokomo, and when she read later that he had been hurt in an accident, she sent a short note to him saying she hoped he was feeling better. Her get well card was returned, opened, with a cryptic note saying personal contact with FBI agents was not allowed.

The Hochstedlers were known to be individualists; they did what they wanted to do and rode with the consequences. But they had hardly ever experienced the isolation and hostility that Jim's draft resistance evoked. Of crucial help to Mary and Milo during this difficult period was John Smucker, a Mennonite pastor in Goshen. His discussions with them helped them cope with the community pressures of having a son who was different and controversial.

Between the time of his arrest at the Alabama commune and his trial, Jim spent more than three months in prison. The bail bond was far too high for Jim to ask anyone to pay, and his lawyer advised that serving some time in prison would help him in court. The federal wardens took their good time transporting Jim from Alabama to Indianapolis for his trial; he stayed in at least five jails during the three weeks they had him on the road. The loneliness of prison reminded him of the isolation he had known while growing up in his home community.

All the other prisoners, in for more typical crimes, thought Jim was going to get off easy since he was a first-time offender. He knew they did not realize how maddening the crime of draft resistance was to those in power. It was his choice to resist and get caught, they figured, and he was not in bad trouble like they were. Jim found that life in prison can become violent at times. Packed elbow to elbow, everyone is forced to relate to each other constantly, whether they want to or not. Some are on edge, ready to fight at the slightest provocation. For everyone, there is the continual threat of homosexual rape. Survival there requires an edgy alertness.

The Indianapolis jail was about a two-hour drive from his folks' place in Kokomo, and they paid regular visits, as did many friends.

At first the guards made Mary talk with Jim through an iron door with small slits five feet up from the floor. She was very short and had a slight hearing problem. It was impossible for her to visit with Jim that way; she could not see him even when she stood on tiptoe, and she had to strain to hear him. After Mary complained to the prison chaplain, they were allowed to talk together in a locked room. During this difficult time, Jim's folks gained comfort from the support of Richard Yoder, the pastor of a local Mennonite church in Indianapolis.

At the arraignment in late July 1971, Jim pleaded guilty to the charge of failure to register. He had no intention of playing a game; he had indeed broken the law and he could not deny that fact without being dishonest. Besides, he had been running from the law and he knew how much that irritated the law-enforcement crowd.

His guilty plea surprised the peace movement crowd that Eli had been part of. Jim-the-Resister was a symbol of what they stood for—people saying no to the government's demands. Pleading guilty, however, was not in character. He had let them down. Many of them had just participated in a big trial in Philadelphia in which a Quaker draft resister, Peter Blood, pleaded not guilty and then called witnesses to testify about the atrocities of the Vietnam War. The judge there had been sympathetic and let Blood go free on a technicality. The peace movement crowd smelled sweet success, and had been ready to rally around hero number two, Jim-the-Resister.

Jim felt their deep disappointment when many of the group came to his trial in a show of personal support. It stirred up mixed emotions inside him. He saw what he thought were sorrowful looks on their faces because he was trampling all over their ideals of right and wrong. But their ideals did not make sense to Jim any more. They thought he should resist to the end, regardless of the consequences. They wanted to act in solidarity as a movement, but he, the individual, had to pay the price alone for the ideals. He was not going to be anybody's martyr substitute anymore; he was not a masochist.

Jim talked with lawyers from the American Civil Liberties Union about taking up his case, but they did not seem to think they could win it, so he dropped his request. The attorney he finally chose came to the case prepared to do whatever he could to get Jim off the hook as much as possible.

Jim worked hard with his attorney to try to encourage the judge to sentence him, not to jail, but to a probationary term of service. The defense team came up with three or four service options in which he could fulfill a probationary sentence. One Mennonite organization, Camp Amigo, where he had worked as a youth, obtained official status as a place for alternative service workers and became an option for the judge in Jim's case.

The day of the trial, August 3, 1971, Jim still had no inkling of what his sentence would be. He was amazed by how quickly the trial went. The FBI failed to appear. The prosecutor spoke very briefly. The judge asked him whether the prosecution had a recommended sentence. "Maximum," said the prosecutor. The judge asked: "Does the prosecution have anything further to say?" "No," came the reply. "Nothing else to say?" queried the judge in surprise. "No," replied the prosecutor.

"Well," said the judge, turning to Jim, "Did they catch you or did you turn yourself in?"

"I was there and they came and got me," replied Jim. The judge made a little speech criticizing draft resistance, and then asked Jim if he had anything else to say. Jim simply stated that he was interested in working, on a probationary term, with one of the several service possibilities he had prepared for the judge.

The judge, one of the more liberal in that jurisdiction, sentenced Jim to two years' probation, working in an area hospital. As the judge voiced the sentence, Jim's parents immediately saw anger in the federal marshalls' faces. The officers were stunned by Jim's light sentence.

Mary and Milo drove Jim home right away. It was the first time he was free in a long time. He went out in the yard—the grass looked so green.

His mom went straight up to the haymow and began pitching bales down the chute. She did not usually do this work, and there were not even any animals around that needed to be fed, but she was so wound up inside that she just had to let off some steam. The tension of the past few months had almost broken her. Like the time at the arraignment, when Mary had been surprised to find herself riding up to the courtroom on the same elevator as the FBI agent who had badgered her for so many months. Politely, she had greeted him and asked how he was. He had avoided looking at her and ignored her question.

Jim soon sat down with the probation officer to work out the details of his service work. A member of Parkview Mennonite had lined up a I-W job for Jim at Kokomo's St. Joseph's Hospital, working as an X-ray orderly.

Then a note arrived in his mailbox, saying he had to register with Selective Service now that he was on probation. His probation officer called and said Jim had five days to register or they would stick him back in jail.

Jim checked around to see if he really had to register. Refusing to register had been the whole point of his resistance in the first place. He could not get anyone to say with certainty that Selective Service could not throw him in jail again, so he decided to forget about it and go register. He made a bit of a joke about it, and scribbled a few wisecracks across the form, but he did fill it out.

Elsie Witmer, his Canadian girl friend, occasionally came down to see him in Kokomo during his probation term. She was shocked by how thin he had become; he looked white from his months in prison. No longer would he voluntarily say what he thought. She had to pry it out of him in private.

After Jim completed his probationary term in Kokomo, he went to Canada again. Elsie and Jim got married in 1974, and began to look for land on which to settle. They spent a few years truck farming on ten acres in central Indiana and then, shopping around for more and cheaper land, they found a re-

mote, 80-acre farm in western Wisconsin and bought it, complete with a barnyard full of cows, manure, and two tractors.

The winters there are raw with wind and snow, the
neighbors few and far between, and the farm in need of
constant care. But it seems a joy for them to work their part of
the earth, secure from issues, troubles, and threats, save those
posed by nature itself. The natural world, with its pastoral
rhythms, appears very friendly.

Now Jim feels he is discovering more and more about
himself and the world. He believes, to avoid unwanted problems, every individual affected should make up his or her own
mind about the draft before conscription. People should be
very definite about it and not talk themselves into a corner
before they are ready. They should decide on their own, or with
someone who will keep his or her mouth shut.

Jim believes potential resisters should entertain no illu-
sions about becoming anything more than temporary heroes.
Everybody else forgets after awhile, but the individual has to
deal with the results for a long time. Potential resisters should
allow others to influence them only as much as the resister
wants, he says, because each resister will end up alone with the
consequences.

If one considers life an adventure, he says, then one will
not regret the experience. That's the way Jim looks at it.

7.

To Not Be the Quiet in the Land

Dan Lehman

*Dan Lehman lives in New York City with his
wife, Barbara Brenneman Lehman. He
works as a political and investigative reporter
for a Brooklyn-based newspaper, and writes
articles for "The Village Voice" and "The
New Yorker."*

Dan was empty. Two years of rowdy living at Goshen College had really drained him, leaving him weary and depressed.

As he muddled through classes during the spring of 1970, he decided—he was going back home to Harrisonburg.

Returning to Virginia was appealing for several reasons. He hated the flat, gray Midwestern terrain of Goshen, Indiana. It just could not match the beauty of Virginia's Shenandoah Valley. His family lived in Harrisonburg, and he wanted to be near them. Plus, Harrisonburg's Eastern Mennonite College (EMC) was a comfortable, secure place—he had practically grown up on the campus. Last, but not least, Barbara would be in Harrisonburg starting her first year of college.

Their dating had begun when Barbara was 14 and he was 16. A deep attraction between them was evident from the beginning, but they had mutually agreed that it would be good for two people so young for Dan to spend some time away in Goshen. It was true that it had been good to be apart, but now Dan wanted to be close to her again.

One of the first things Dan did when he returned home that summer was to enroll with Barbara in a seminar on Christian peacemaking that was being held at EMC. The thrust of the seminar was on radical Christianity, a Christ-centered life that emphasized active and vocal opposition to the evil it encounters in the world. Dan had always considered himself a political radical; for the first time he was hearing about a faith he could believe in with integrity. It occurred to him that perhaps all the emptiness and confusion that he had felt during the last few years was a result of not believing in Christ. The seminar's study book, *The New Left and Christian Radicalism,* by Art Gish, whetted Dan's appetite and provoked new thoughts.

His new experience of Christianity coincided with his consideration of draft resistance. He had begun to see the inequities of the draft. It was so easy for him to get the conscientious objector's status, just by virtue of his Mennonite heritage. But during the previous year at Goshen, he had seen a friend of his drafted who was a "town kid," a non-Mennonite who did not have the easy way out. His friend was enroute to Vietnam, and Dan was afraid for him.

His concern about the war was fueled by the news that four college students had been shot to death by National Guardsmen on the campus of Ohio's Kent State University. Young people were being killed on the campuses as well as on the battlefields.

He tried out his thoughts about radical Christianity on Barbara. Talking with her was always easy. One night, as they stood on the steps of the women's residence hall on campus, he sensed it beginning to come together. Religion for him had always meant being good, being careful, toeing the line. On the other hand, all his inclinations were to do the unacceptable things. He was not one of the quiet in the land. Before, religious impulses had always served to drag him back into being quiet and conservative—following the rules. But now, he explained to Barbara, he saw in Christianity the potential for radicalism, for not toeing the line, for taking controversial stands. It was not a simplistic, come-into-my-heart-Jesus conversion, but it nevertheless was an important moment of conversion for Dan.

Barbara listened to him carefully. She was excited about his experience. It was the closest thing to faith she had ever heard him express. One of her earliest impressions of him was a time when he spoke, along with a few other students, about his most meaningful church experience. Dan's speech had been unique—he had not had a meaningful church experience, he said, and explained why. Now he was seeing meaning and worth in Christianity, and for that she was happy. One thing troubled her though. What would her dad think about Dan's conversion to a radical Christianity?

Barbara's father, Fred Brenneman, was a psychiatrist. Of concern to Dan and Barbara, though, was the fact that he was a Mennonite minister staunchly committed to the principle of nonconformity. For Dr. Brenneman, nonconformity meant a distinct separation from the world, and certain concrete things—like prayer coverings for women, abstinence from alcohol and tobacco, and modest clothing—were the essential marks of nonconformity. But what would he think of draft resistance? Might he see it as conformity to the hippie generation?

Barbara and Dan got the opportunity to test the waters with Fred and Millie Brenneman later that summer while Dan was visiting Barbara's home in Pennsylvania. The subject of draft resistance came up in the conversation, at first rather abstractly, with everyone casually offering opinions. But Dan, defending the resistance position, found his emotions rising, and spontaneously blurted out, "I personally see a lot of value in that response to the draft. In fact, I'm considering it myself."

An abrupt, heavy silence fell over the room. Everyone was a bit shocked. Then the discussion began again and continued for several hours, this time on a more personal note with Dan as the focus of the questions. When Dan left at the end of the weekend, he did not feel badly about the conversations. He had been respected, and Barbara's father had perhaps even understood his reasoning.

In the meantime, Dan's commitment to Christianity involved another action. Some young Mennonites had recently taken over a church service in Goshen to talk about peace. Dan and Barbara, along with Ed Bumbaugh and Curt Berkey, decided to carry out a similar action at Park View, Dan's home church in Harrisonburg.

They were going to be very prepared. The four agreed that they did not want to take over the church and "just spout their line." Rather, they wanted to try to speak to the church in its own terminology. So, they began their summer in intensive Bible study. They bought copies of the *Good News for Modern Man* Bible, and read it from cover to cover. Then they studied the entire text, especially focusing on everything that seemed politically radical. For Dan, the Bible became richly alive. Whereas before he had slept through readings of the Scripture, now he was excited. The book of James, the Sermon on the Mount, other teachings of Christ—all these passages leaped from the pages and challenged him in his new faith.

By July, the four felt they were ready. When they tipped-off the pastor, Harold Eshleman, he surprised them by his open acceptance of their proposal. He agreed to give them an entire Sunday morning to do whatever they wanted.

The group, which had humorously designated themselves the Park View Action Faction, laid careful plans. Dan would deliver the sermon; the others would talk briefly.

When the day arrived, all went as scheduled. Dan opened his talk with the query: "When someone mentions Park View Church, do you think of brick, mortar, red carpet, padded benches, and a substantial debt? Or do you think of a committed unit of Christians denying comforts of this world and taking up the cross in intense love and servanthood to the world at large?"

His question set the tone for his entire talk. After a systematic look at related scriptural references, Dan acknowledged his own failings. "When we first considered this meeting one and a half months ago, I was going to speak from a self-righteous standpoint. But after studying God's Word and praying, I now hang my head when I think how far I am from the ideal of Christ's message. My father can and will tell you of my materialism, my record collection, my appetite, my rash anger, and my foolish deeds."

He closed with an appeal to the church that they meet as a congregation "to question the whole validity of our structure. If we are serious in our desire to reflect a divine Christ," he said, "then we must submit ourselves to his will even if it means, as it did for the rich young ruler, that we must sell our possessions, even our church building, and give the money to the poor. We may not be asked to go this far but we must be ready to examine ourselves to that extent, or we have lost our vision as a brotherhood of believers."

Dan's parents, Harold and Ruth Lehman, were proud of him. His mom especially was thrilled that he had found a meaningful faith. Of course, she worried about his talk of draft resistance—he was even thinking of emigrating to Canada—but she would deal with that when it became more pressing.

After Dan's sermon, the offering was taken. But then the young people in charge sent the collection plate back into the congregation, telling people to take out what they needed. Of course no one took any money. One of the four then stood up and said, "Do you realize that this might say something about us? It seems like we aren't really giving where it hurts."

When the church service had ended, the four young people were invited to continue their discussion with the congregation during the Sunday school hour. At some point during the church service, Dan had spoken about his resistance plans. That turned out to be the "hot" subject. Dan, being the one who had mentioned the subject in the first place, had most of the questions directed to him. Although Dan was unaccustomed to defending himself on theological matters, he had to when some of the church members vigorously challenged him. Being publicly challenged on his personal stance was a new and difficult experience for Dan.

As the hour drew to a halt, somebody had one last thing to ask of Dan. "Don't you feel that as a Mennonite, this important decision can't be made on your own? Don't you think that you should submit your decision to the body of believers?"

"Yes," Dan agreed. "From an Anabaptist perspective, a community of believers is very important. But if, on the other hand, the early Anabaptists had only been concerned about reaching consensus, they would have stayed in their monasteries," he said, as he slowed, uncertain about his ancestors' origins, . . . "or wherever they came from."

Someone suggested a follow-up meeting with the church and the would-be resisters, and everyone agreed. Dan and a guy named George Lehman, who was also considering resistance, agreed to meet, and the following Monday night was set as a suitable time.

D an's parents made sure they were at church the following night. They did not exactly see eye to eye with him on this subject, but they felt it was important to support him. Dan was glad for their presence.

Those Sunday and Monday night meetings were crucial for Dan. Of course, nobody changed anybody's mind. But it provided Dan with an opportunity to focus his feelings. In later years, Dan thought that it was important for an even bigger reason. It had been his first public stand. He had been looking for a unique identity, and becoming a draft resister was one way of achieving that.

After investing five hours at the church and an immeasurable amount of emotional energy, he was increasingly ready to resist. His parents had indicated that they would stand behind him, especially his mother. It was harder for Dan to figure out his dad's thinking.

Part of Ruth's understanding grew out of her job, working in the registrar's office at EMC during the Vietnam War. She may have had the toughest assignment on campus; it was her responsibility to handle all the dealings with the FBI over student resisters' records. Gradually, Ruth had begun to feel that EMC was cooperating too much with the FBI.

She questioned her boss. "Do you really think we ought to be allowing the FBI such free access to our files?" She explained why she thought they should not. The registrar assured her that he would check into it.

Several days later the word came back to her. He had checked with the dean, and they had agreed. It was fair and reasonable to cooperate with the FBI. She was encouraged to continue her responsibilities as before. She followed orders, but she still wondered. Weren't she and EMC helping the government fight the Vietnam War?

By the time her son began considering resistance, she understood his position. She also recognized the painful irony of her position. Because of her job, she would be asked to cooperate with the FBI in building a case against her son, an EMC student! It did cross her mind that she could voluntarily turn Dan's name in to the FBI, so that Dan would receive the student deferment. But that was not what Dan wanted. She had enough respect for her son not to interfere in his plans. The day the FBI called though, asking if she knew Daniel Wayne Lehman, she put the call on hold and transferred it over to her boss.

Dan knew his resisting was considerably more difficult for

his dad to accept. He had a great deal of respect for his dad. Harold Lehman was very committed to the conscientious objection movement. He had held a position of leadership during the early days of the Civilian Public Service program. Harold maintained that alternative service was a commendable and valuable way to respond to the government's demands.

His discussions with Dan were filled with challenging questions. He wanted Dan to make a rational, well-thought-out choice. For one thing, he questioned whether the resisters were acting out of some sort of guilt complex. Second, Harold felt that some older members of the movement—men who had completed their alternative service before they became politicized—were using the younger fellows. He thought it quite possible that the older ones were acting like generals, turning people like Dan into fodder for the front lines.

But when all the long talks were over and he realized that Dan's decision was final, Harold showed support in small but definite ways. As soon as he heard the four young people were going to lead a service at Park View, he approached Dan and his friends, offering to lead the singing. He knew they would want to have singing and none of them were choristers.

But while Dan felt secure in knowing his parents supported him, and while Barbara agreed that he should resist, he knew his resistance certainly could change his and Barbara's future. With his low lottery number, he would surely be on the government's "hit list." Dan figured that he did not have much choice when it came to handling the consequences of his resistance. Prison was definitely out of the question; he had decided early on that he did not have the mental or emotional fortitude for such an experience. Canada, then, became his only option. Through discussions with Mennonite Central Committee, he worked out a tentative position with them in Toronto.

But would Barbara be allowed to follow? She was still quite young, just out of high school. If their relationship was going to grow, they would need the Brenneman family's support. Would her parents encourage an increasingly serious relationship with a draft resister?

All his thinking, talking with other people, and wondering how folks would react did not change the fact that it was his own hard, lonely decision to make for himself. He chose to resist.

On August 12, 1970, he wrote a letter to his draft board.

D ear friends," he began. "I speak to you as fellow humans. I do not speak to you as a draft board because I can no longer recognize the validity of the function that you serve. However, I choose to write to you as persons because I feel I have a duty as a fellow human being to witness of my decision of affirmation for human life.

"This affirmation is in obedience to the command of Christ, my personal leader, to love my neighbor as myself. Christ tells us specifically that our neighbors include our enemies, that we should not resist them with force but rather show them respect and love. I have come to the realization that if we as human beings ever come to the point where we practice peace on earth, it will be because we live peace on earth now in response to the call of Christ.

"Therefore, to obey Christ and affirm life, I must refuse to cooperate with any system that affirms death. The Selective Service System is, I feel, an integral part of a violent system. I can no longer recognize its validity or the function of my local draft board. For this reason I have returned my registration and classification cards. Moreover, I shall counsel others to reevaluate their own response to a system which affirms death.

"I hope you will understand I bear no malice to you as persons but I must reject your control over my life as a draft board. I am fully aware of the consequences this decision may have for my future but I am secure in the knowledge that I am responding in obedience to Christ.

"My cards are at your disposal. I have no more use for them. I am sorry things had to work out this way between us, but I hope we can maintain love for each other as persons. Feel free to contact me on a person-to-person basis in the future if you wish to discuss my position. I remain always your brother and sincerely hope my stand will help you to re-evaluate your own cooperation with a violent system."

He signed it, "In brotherly love and peace."

With the letter in the mail, Dan's thoughts turned to what it might mean for him to break the law. By now, Barbara and he were definitely headed toward marriage. But the fall of 1970 was not the time to announce their engagement; they wanted their relationship, and themselves, to age a bit first. They also wanted to plan their lives together and Dan's resistance made planning difficult. How would Barbara's parents respond?

The Brennemans came through with a solid commitment of support. In the early fall, they drove to Harrisonburg and took Barbara and Dan out to the town's "nice" restaurant—Lloyd's Steakhouse. Over dinner, Fred Brenneman said he did not believe that resistance was a necessary tenet of the Anabaptist position. But he also said that, from a nonconformist's perspective, Dan's response to the draft was valid, worthy of respect and support.

After a long discussion, they agreed; Barbara could go to Waterloo, Ontario, to study at the Mennonite-run Conrad Grebel College there, if things got to that point, so that she could be close to Dan in Canada. They would continue to provide financially for her education.

Dan was elated. He had successfully communicated with his future in-laws. Plus, by their support, the Brennemans were offering their tacit acceptance of Dan and Barbara's unannounced plans to marry.

But riding home in the car, Dan felt things turn sour. Dr. Brenneman was talking about resistance and nonconformity, and somehow was winding the conversation around to modesty and prayer coverings and how necessary it was for the church to return to those essential doctrines.

Dan felt crushed. As he bid the Brennemans good night at the car and walked to his door, he wondered how soon it would be before he found himself wearing a plain coat and toeing the line, playing the nonconformist. Did draft resistance really mean doing all these things?

He soon heard from the draft board. Their reaction to his carefully composed, sincere letter was to suddenly reclassify him as I-A, available for military service. He was stunned. How could they so drastically misunderstand his position?

Dan turned to his pastor, Harold Eshleman, for help. "Would you be willing to go with me to the draft board just to make sure they really hear what I think?" he asked.

"Certainly," came his pastor's unhesitating reply, and Dan secured a hearing date with the busy draft board, a few months ahead. He knew that Harold Eshleman would be a good man to have along as a pastor in such a situation. His active commitment to community work resulted in many contacts and respect with the general citizenry of the community.

The autumn began to fill with bittersweet memories. Believing that emigration to Canada would be permanent, he enjoyed the sumptuous beauty of the Virginia countryside for what he imagined to be the last time. On Sunday afternoons he and Barbara would borrow his parents' car and drive into the mountains which defined the valley. Longingly he would gaze out over the hills, trying to etch the scene into his memory. He did not want to leave, but he believed it was necessary; his conscience bid him do so. Each football game he watched brought the same feeling. This could be his last autumn in Virginia ever; a part of him was always grieving.

Christmas. Would he ever again spend Christmas in his parents' home? Lighter moments came also, like when his parents gave him ice skates as a Christmas present. "You'll need them in Canada," they joked.

Christmas 1970 was the date he and Barbara had picked to announce their engagement. Conscious of their youthfulness, they told their parents they would not get married for another year or so.

Dan's hearing took place in January 1971. It was held on the second floor of the Harrisonburg post office, in a room heavy with somber gray-green paint and institutional furniture.

Dan took in the four representatives of the draft board with a quick glance—the female clerk and three older males. The men looked quite serious. I bet they get along just fine with Mennonites, Dan thought, because Mennonites are quiet. They don't make a fuss. They just stay to themselves in their parts of the country.

The draft board officials were not certain about how to deal with Dan, this not-so-quiet Mennonite. His demeanor and replies were subdued, respectful. But his refusal to carry a draft card, that they could not understand. Their initial plan was to deal with it quickly.

Having requested the hearing, Dan was allowed to speak first. "As I mentioned in my letter," he said, "I don't really think of you as a draft board anymore. I requested the hearing because I think you misread my letter completely by classifying

me as I-A. If you misunderstood my position, then I must conclude that you might misread other people's positions." He
continued on for several minutes, explaining why he had
returned his draft cards.

After a few exchanges of questions and answers between
Dan and the draft board, one man said, "Well, if you're a
student, are you going to ask for a student deferment?"

"No," Dan replied.

"You know you'll be drafted. We have you classified as I-
A, so you're going to be inducted and if you don't step forward
when you're called to be inducted, you'll be arrested."

Dan offered no response.

The three officials looked at each other. One sighed
heavily. Another asked Dan, "Have you said everything to us
that you want?"

"Yes."

"We've said everything that we can, so we might as well
. . . oh, excuse me, Reverend Eshleman, is there anything that
you would like to add?"

The pastor spoke briefly about the sincerity of Dan's commitment, indicating that he could vouch that Dan was returning
his draft card as a matter of conscience. Perhaps he was speaking more favorably of me than he actually believes, Dan
thought, but the support was invaluable.

Then everything was over. Everyone had had their say—
there seemed to be nothing more to do. In fact, they had all
reached for their jackets when one official, the guy who had
been the most pleasant, said, "Look, there has to be some alternative to this kind of thing. Dan, do you really want to go
through with this? Why don't we look at it again, there might be
a way out."

All settled back into their chairs, and a long discussion
followed. Instead of both sides restating their positions, they

began asking questions of each other, trying to understand their seemingly incompatible differences.

The draft board men asked him specific questions about his beliefs, and then told him in greater detail why they thought he was wrong. They talked a lot about World War II; all three of them had served in the military, two of them during World War II. One of the guys had even lost part of a leg in the war. Although the draft board members made a few comments like, "We're the ones who protect pacifists like you," in general, the tone was rather deferential to the Mennonite position, likely because a well-respected Mennonite minister was sitting there, Dan thought.

The meeting went on for another two and a half hours. Several times, Dan was offered the opportunity to change his mind. Everyone was seated around a large table, with Dan and his pastor on one side and the draft officials on the other. The draft board wanted Dan to request a student deferment. It was clear that they did not want to send him to prison, but he was breaking the law, a fact they could not simply ignore.

Over and over again, as they sat around the large, wooden table, they would say, "Why don't you just sign the paper, Dan? You really don't want to go to prison, do you?" And then one of the officials would shove the paper across the table until it was lying under Dan's nose.

Each time, Dan would look at it a while. It was a simple form, a request for a student deferment. Would it really matter if he took the student deferment which was technically fair and certainly legal? But no, he did not want to cooperate with the Selective Service System in any way. Firmly resolved, he would thrust the paper away and say, "I'm not going to sign it."

Another round of discussion would follow, with the request form again ending up in front of Dan. Each time he paused to consider. Each time he decided no.

Finally all of them grew tired. They had talked long enough to know that Dan's position would not be weakened. An alternative could not be found. They wearily pushed back their chairs and again reached for their jackets.

Then one of the draft board men spoke. He had been acting in the "bad-guy" role during the entire hearing. "As I see it," the words came slowly, "we're going to have to give you a 2-S classification. It seems to me that you're a confused boy. You're obviously a student, and students are permitted a deferment under the Selective Service law. So, I'm not sure how we'll do it, but we'll get a signature somehow and give you that student deferment for a year. Maybe a year from now you won't be so confused."

Dan was certainly confused at the moment. What had the guy said? Everybody else in the room seemed so happy. His pastor, Harold Eshleman, was slapping him on the back and the other two officials were smiling. The tension had been eased, but what was the guy saying now?

"One little thing," the guy said. "Here are your draft cards. Why don't you take them? We don't want them cluttering up our files. Here you go." And he held them out to Dan.

Dan looked at Harold, uncertain. Harold, with a friendly shrug seemed to say, "They've helped you out." So Dan picked up his cards.

Then he was out the door into the crisp winter air and, in a short while, back home. The first thing he did was find Barbara. He was not prepared for her reaction.

"Dan, I'm glad you don't have to go to Canada and that we can stay here. But how could you take the cards? That was your way of resisting—returning your cards. And now here they are. It just seems like you didn't stand up to them at all."

Dan was still confused. He did not really understand what had happened in the post office building. He didn't want the draft cards and he didn't want to cooperate with the Selective Service System. But at the time, taking the cards had not seemed like such a horrendous act.

He and Barbara argued back and forth for a long time. Hours later they were sitting on a swing at a friend's place. Dan had torn up his draft cards. But they were both still upset and frustrated, feeling like the draft board had tricked him. As they sat there, a deep calmness came over them. In an instant, their spirits lightened and they began to feel much better. Dan would later say that it was a rare mystical experience.

In August, Dan and Barbara were married. By that time, Dan was again looking at his relationship with the Selective Service System. His year's reprieve was almost at an end. He began to consider the possibilities. As before, prison just could not be an option. Again he checked out Canada. Mennonite Central Committee (MCC) offered him a position, this time in Winnipeg, Manitoba.

Other factors colored his decision-making. He had grown more interested in issues concerning the United States and was increasingly aware of his own fascination with American politics. He would be an uninformed foreigner if he moved to Canada. By what right would he ever be able to get involved in the politics of another country?

Something else was affecting him. Dan knew a guy who was vehemently against the war. He had already completed the required amount of alternative service, but he encouraged Dan's resistance. In one conversation Dan asked him if he would consider returning his draft cards. Likely he would not experience any bad consequences; it would simply be a show of support for young guys like Dan. The guy agreed to mail back his cards but Dan found out that he never actually mailed them. Wondering why he had not, Dan felt let down and used.

With his decision unsettled, Dan went to an MCC meeting in St. Louis, as a representative of EMC's student peace club, of which he was the president. What he saw there he did not like. He sensed that the Mennonite draft resistance movement was splitting into two factions.

One element he saw as back-to-the-earth, radical promoters of the simple lifestyle. They seemed to be defining their Anabaptism as returning to a simplistic, withdrawal existence. Dan was put off by what he thought was their harsh righteousness. Live a pure life and you'll get to heaven, they seemed to say. Dan began to think—it is a very fine line that separates steadfastness and rigidity, that separates flexibility and wishy-washyness. He began to conclude that he did not want to spend all his life trying so hard to be right.

Dan identified more closely with the other faction—mostly young urbanites, holding positions like minister, church worker, or Voluntary Service unit leader. Most important to him, these were the people involved in the front lines of community organization work.

Dan began to wonder if he really wanted to go to Canada and be a guy who never compromised, who was never tainted by evil. Maybe instead he wanted to go to a United States city where he might get a little tainted but still could be involved in something meaningful and worthwhile.

He carried his questions back to Barbara. A long disagreement followed. She felt strongly that it was a time for no compromises with the government and she did not understand Dan's shift. Part of Dan's changing viewpoint involved his feelings about Christianity. Before he resisted, he had never reinforced his political beliefs with the moral absolutes of right and wrong. The period from June 1970 until the following autumn was the only time he had placed his personal decisions within such a context. Now Dan was just not sure he could believe that anything held absolute truth.

Therefore, while opposing the war in Vietnam was still important to him politically and morally, he was no longer motivated to resist the draft for reasons of religious nonconformity.

If he was not resisting the draft for religious reasons, then why was he, he asked? If he considered the political implications, it was true that draft resistance had had significant political effects. The protest movement, he believed, had been instrumental in forcing the government to reconsider its role in Vietnam. But by the fall of 1971, the war seemed to be de-escalating, and Dan questioned what effect his individual resistance could have. If he spent the rest of his life in Canada, how would that in any way be relevant to the ongoing U.S. political situation?

What it boiled down to was a choice between moving to Manitoba or accepting the student deferment. Moving away from family and everything familiar seemed like a senseless way to protest the war, so he decided to accept the student deferment. It took some time and much convincing to get Barbara on board, but eventually she accepted his decision.

I t was the first year of their marriage but it was not a particularly happy one. They were constantly struggling with heavy decisions, like whether or not to emigrate to Canada. In addition, both of them were going to college full time, and their heavy involvement with the peace club drained time and energy. They definitely needed some fun and lightness in their lives.

John Suter, one of Dan's old high school buddies who lived in Florida, visited Dan and Barbara several times in the fall of that year. Each time he came, he melted some of their tension with his relaxed spirit and good-times air.

John encouraged them to come down to Florida to visit him, and they took him up on his offer during their weeklong break in late February 1972. Boy, did they have a good time. Restaurants, the beach, dancing, and just sitting around talking and laughing. Both Dan and Barbara came home from the vacation thinking the same thoughts. They were not going to spend their whole lives being so serious and committed that they could not have any fun.

Dan graduated in the spring of 1972. An EMC friend, Mel Lehman, talked to him about the two of them starting a neighborhood newspaper in Washington, D.C. The idea appealed to Dan. It would involve some writing, some politics, and hopefully, the community organizing that he found intriguing. The autumn of 1972 found Dan and Barbara in Washington.

A notice arrived from his draft board. He had graduated and his student deferment was no longer valid. The letter indicated that he had been drafted in the nation's final draft.

Dan was feeling much stronger by now, more able to deal decisively with the draft board and the draft. He was still involved with the neighborhood newspaper, *The Columbian*, and he decided he would try to continue working there.

He talked to the folks at MCC. Previously he had been impressed with their commitment and support. He sounded them out on an idea for dealing with the draft board's demands. He would continue to work on *The Columbian* staff, and MCC would indicate to his draft board that he was working for them in an alternative service assignment. MCC agreed, and in communications with Dan's draft board, MCC referred to his job as being an "out of the office" one. Dan had no further dealings with his draft board.

The second thing he did was report for his physical. He decided to go just for the experience. It left a vivid impression with him for a long time. The other inductees who traveled with him on the bus got rowdily drunk to forget the cutting irony of their being caught in the last draft. They reminded him of a friend of his who had gone to Vietnam in the military and picked up a heroin addiction in the process. Dan had an alternative service out; these other guys did not. The least he was able to do was to talk to a few of them about what he was doing and why. He told them how they could apply for CO status, and they seemed interested.

D an and Barbara remained in Washington for five years. Dan worked on the newspaper and later attended graduate school. Barbara finished an elementary education degree and then began teaching. When she decided to attend graduate school in 1977, they moved to New York City. There Barbara completed a master's degree program and then resumed her work as a teacher. Dan continued his writing as a political and investigative reporter.

Today, Dan gains a great deal of satisfaction from his journalism work, believing that his efforts to expose political corruption in New York City and encourage justice through his articles are consistent with his earlier resistance to the political injustice of the draft. Dan hopes that his current job with a community newspaper will eventually land him full-time work with one of the established magazines.

Dan sees his draft resistance as an act of courage, but also as a statement of his coming-of-age period. If he were counseling nineteen-year-olds about resistance, he says, "Although I support resistance and oppose the draft, I would spend weeks talking to them, challenging their motives, questioning them. I clarified my beliefs most when people challenged me."

8.

Who Is Like unto God?

Walter Hochstetler

Walter Hochstetler lives at the Fellowship of Hope Community in Elkhart, Indiana, with his wife, Frances Zerger Hochstetler, and their two children. He is a social worker for the St. Joseph's County welfare program. He also serves as a music minister for the fellowship and as a member of their pastoral team.

At age twenty-five Walter was older than most draft resisters. While studying in the late 1960s at the Mennonite seminary in Goshen, Indiana, he had come into close contact with younger students at the nearby Mennonite college who had already resisted or were thinking about taking that action.

Walter's desire to resist was simple but deep. As a Christian, he tried to closely follow the teachings of Jesus in all aspects of his life and especially longed to be a peacemaker. Shocked by the horror of the Vietnam War, he viewed the American military presence in Southeast Asia as an ugly, evil cancer.

In an agonizing struggle of conscience, he deliberated over how he might best protest the war. One option was to return his draft cards as a symbolic statement of his opposition to war; and on the positive side, as a reflection of his support for peace. He was mulling over this option during the summer of 1969 when he received the news that his nephew Wilbur had been killed in a horrible car wreck.

Wilbur had been a bright, talented young man of eighteen, with plans to enter the Mennonite Church's Voluntary Service program. In the middle of the summer, Wilbur had received a notice from the draft board. Mistakenly classified, he took off work during his lunch hour to correct the error. While driving to the draft board, he had the fatal car accident.

When Walter heard the news of his nephew's death, he seethed with anger. Wilbur's death symbolized the ineptitude and wrongness of the draft board. Because of their mismanagement, Wilbur had lost his life. Meanwhile, by their efficient management, thousands of drafted young Americans, as well as Vietnamese, were dying.

For Walter, this was the last straw. His nephew was not a

resister, but he had died because of the draft board. In response, Walter decided he had to risk his life to oppose all that the draft board stood for; he would have to become a non-cooperator with the draft and devote his life to the cause of peace.

After Wilbur's death, questions about the meaning of Christianity swelled within Walter. Maybe death is the end of everything, he pondered. If a young promising life like Wilbur's could be snuffed out, then perhaps life itself was senseless and absurd.

Institutional Christianity seemed to be bankrupt, what with its silent, unquestioning support of the government's military policies in Vietnam. Even though Walter was excited about Anabaptism, he questioned the commitment of the Mennonite churches compared to their sixteenth-century radical Reformation ancestors.

Somehow, in the midst of his doubts, a spark of faith remained. Jesus' teachings, which he considered the core of Christianity, continued to inspire him. The institutional church might well be on the wrong track, but Walter knew it was up to him alone to decide whether he was going to follow Jesus or not.

Within two weeks of Wilbur's death, Walter returned his draft card. In an accompanying letter to his draft board, he listed his arguments against the draft:

"First, the draft is unconstitutional: it is an explicit form of 'involuntary servitude.' It demands slave labor in the most inhuman kind of work. Furthermore the draft coerces people to participate in the cultic worship of the American folk religion. The constitution forbids the establishment of any such national religion.

"Second, the draft system is inhuman. Because it channels men into the armed forces, it helps to cheapen the value of human life and destroy the profound respect for the sanctity of human life (life was also said to be an 'inalienable right' in the Declaration of Independence). It is depersonalizing because it claims that institutions are more important than persons. It is dehumanizing, for men are taught to regard their brothers as enemies and to slaughter them if they happen to dislike our way of policing the world.

"Third, the draft is a tool for the perpetuation of the myths on which America is built. That we are a free country is simply not true for millions of Americans who are trapped in poverty and in racial ghettos. The escalation of the repression of dissent betrays the totalitarian character of an insecure government. Neither can America claim (if indeed this was ever the case) that we are the 'moral leaders' of the world. Our exploitative capitalism and aggressive militarism are the most immoral of any nation in the world.

"A further objection to the draft would be its discriminatory character. The poor and the blacks are particularly victimized by this form of prostitution. On the other hand, white, middle (and upper) class—and I might add, students, and particularly ministerial students and ministers—find it much easier to get deferments and exemptions. Thus I protest this kind of unwarranted, privileged status."

Walter's parents, Elam and Elsie Hochstetler, did not play an active role in his resistance, although he believed that they had planted in him the seeds of nonviolence during his childhood. Although he did not talk much about it with them, he did not sense that his parents were strongly opposed to his draft resistance. They had joined the Beachy Amish Church in Indiana when he was young. He had left that church to become a Mennonite in 1966 and the two sister traditions had merged into a powerful peace influence in his life. Being away at school, at a Mennonite college and a Mennonite seminary, had distanced him from the Beachy Amish church and put some miles, both physical and emotional, between himself and his parents.

His family had been supportive of alternative service; two brothers and a sister of his had worked in Voluntary Service. Walter respected people who chose that route, but increasingly he felt that alternative service programs like VS were too closely connected with the government's Selective Service System, and that Selective Service was simply an arm of the American military.

When the historic peace churches had negotiated years before with the government to establish the alternative service program, Walter figured that the government officials assumed the alternative service classification would keep Mennonites quiet and encourage them to ignore wars. It seemed to Walter that the government had tried to buy off the pacifists.

Not that Walter had anything against Voluntary Service or I-W alternative service. In fact, he had volunteered to go into VS at one earlier point, but no concrete assignment had materialized. It was just that he feared alternative service provided the government with an easy opportunity to sooth dissenters, discouraging criticism of the military.

To him, the whole purpose of the Selective Service System, designed to provide manpower for the military, could be summed up in the words "death and destruction." A few people were given exemptions, but only so that the system could function with little disruption. By accepting an exemption, Walter felt he would be an accomplice in the death-murders caused by Selective Service. God had called him to be a peacemaker; he would not take part in any branch of the military.

Walter tried to be very clear with the draft board, indicating that he would not accept his draft cards and would refuse to report for induction if drafted. In the exchange of letters with the draft board that followed, the government was less than responsive. Its first reply indicated that it had received his letter, said that his action was in violation of the Selective Service Act, and offered to issue duplicate cards if he wished to reconsider.

Little happened for about half a year. But in January 1970, while a seminary student, he received word that he had been reclassified I-0, a classification that meant the draft board considered him eligible to be ordered into alternative service. With his low lottery number in the draft—14—Walter was a sitting duck; it was guaranteed that he would be inducted now, even though he was a student and students were supposed to be exempted from induction.

Walter strongly suspected that the new classification had been imposed to harass him. The draft board wanted to punish him for not carrying his draft cards, and this was the fastest way to nail him. He mailed the classification papers back along with the new cards, saying they were unacceptable. He would definitely not make himself available for any officially approved civilian service contributing to the "national health, safety, or interest." At the same time, he sent the draft board copies of the Mennonite Church's statement, passed at Turner, Oregon, in 1969, that condoned draft resistance.

Walter had earlier found a great deal of support in the Mennonite Church for resistance, especially in individuals like John A. Lapp, Harold Regier, and Walt Hackman at the 1969 Mennonite Central Committee Peace Section consultation on the draft in Chicago. He heard the older Mennonites at the consultation say that the agenda of the church and its members should be to first discern the will of God and then deal with the demands of the government. If the government's call conflicted with God's, one should follow God and let the chips fall where they may.

The congregation Walter was attending in 1970, Campus Church in Goshen, provided some affirmation, although they took no official action on his behalf. He drew strength from fellowshiping with his small "k-group" of eight seminarians. Two others in this group were considering draft resistance too.

V oices beyond the Mennonite Church inspired him as well. Fathers Dan and Phil Berrigan deeply moved him when they destroyed the draft board files in Catonsville, Maryland, in protest against the war. It seemed to Walter that their action was one more important way that people were saying yes to life and no to death.

He was growing more and more excited about draft resistance, increasingly compelled to talk about his convictions with others. So, in a letter to the draft board, he requested a hearing on his case. Walter especially viewed his privileged position as a religious conscientious objector with chagrin, knowing that people opposed to the war for other than religious reasons usually ended up being forced to go into the military.

The local draft board refused to allow a hearing and reconsider his I-O classification, forcing him to turn to the state appeals board. Walter was afraid that the reclassification refusal would lead to a quick, easy prosecution of him. The draft board members would order him to report for induction. If he did not report, they would have clear grounds for prosecution. If he did appear, which they no doubt considered unlikely, given his previous correspondence, they would order him into alternative service which they knew he would likely refuse, likewise giving them an excuse to prosecute him.

In his appeal to the state board, Walter referred to the recent Supreme Court ruling in which local draft boards were stripped of the power to speed up the induction of young men who turned in their draft cards to protest the Vietnam War. Apparently that ruling convinced somebody. The state board mailed him new cards, reclassifying him again as IV-D, the exemption given to seminarians. Its attitude seemed to be: you're in seminary, so we're going to give you this exemption whether you want it or not.

Walter had mixed feelings about his reclassification. He had hoped to be granted a hearing in which he would ask the board to classify him as II-S, the general deferment for students. Somehow, by this time he felt it was more acceptable to take a II-S deferment than the one specifically for seminary students. But since he was to graduate from seminary in a few months anyway, he decided to let the matter ride.

In June 1970, the local draft board sent him a questionnaire requesting updated information. At that point, he wanted to maintain a total noncooperation stance, so he returned the form uncompleted. He suspected that the draft board was after him because of his resistance. It responded with a reminder that an induction notice could follow shortly unless he filled out the questionnaire. Although Walter expected the draft board to take quick action because of his resistance, as well as his low lottery number, the summer passed without further incident.

The summer was a time of difficult decision-making. Should he stay out of seminary in the fall, lose his student deferment, and likely get drafted, so that he could refuse induction and thereby have a better opportunity to confront the government? Or should he remain in school and finish his degree, while at the same time turn 26 years old and be too old for the draft? There was no choice that seemed clearly right.

After much prayer and talking with friends, he decided to go back to seminary. He felt God wanted him to be in Elkhart, continuing his involvement with the Fellowship of Hope, a newly formed Christian community, and it seemed right to be finishing his degree at the seminary.

After his seminary courses finished in December 1970, he helped to stage a local rally called "The War Is Over." The organizers took their cue from an incident in the War of 1812 when General Andrew Jackson's troops continued to fight after the war was over because they had not received the news that it had ended. Leafleting, media blitzes, and a celebration rally were used to announce that, although the American government had not noticed, the Vietnam War was over.

He sent some of the rally's promotional material to his local draft board, again requesting a hearing. He wanted to address the members of the draft board directly, as fellow human beings, to speak to them of his struggle to try to be a faithful Christian in a country that was waging an unjust war. In addition, he planned to talk critically about the privileged status of seminary students, and indicate that he was no longer in school and ready to accept any consequences that this might mean.

Although he was 26 by that time, and technically did not have a legal reason to call for a hearing, he was granted one, set for June 1, 1971. A group of people gathered with him at the local draft board, but they were not allowed to be in the room where the hearing was held. Their songs of peace wafted through the walls from the hallway outside, however, and Walter was comforted as their presence intruded in on the proceedings. The singing bothered the draft board members though, and that proved to be a bit amusing. The officials would intermittently send someone out into the hall to tell the serenaders of peace to quiet down or move farther away.

Walter had a great deal to tell the draft board; they had very little to say in return. With urgency, he tried to state that he felt God was calling people like himself, the five draft board members, indeed, all of America, to follow the Prince of Peace, because he was the Christ, the Son of God. The Selective Service System and its purposes were diametrically opposed to his understanding of the gospel.

Walter concluded by handing them his draft cards, stained with a few drops of his blood. He knew it was a dramatic, extreme act, but he wanted to leave them with a very real symbol of life and portray his willingness to shed his own blood rather than to shed anyone else's. He saw it as a sacrificial sign of his readiness to suffer rather than inflict suffering on others. It was also a way of bringing home some of the blood of Vietnam to representatives of the Selective Service System that kept sending men off to fight. He wanted to confront them with the results of their work.

The members of the draft board showed little response as he handed the blood-spotted cards to them. He imagined that they were at least a little repulsed. Several of them commented that he was being irrational, or too radical, but little else was said. The next day, they sent him another card with a I-O classification, apparently having decided that further debate would not serve any useful purpose.

During that year, he demonstrated his peacemaking in a more unusual way. Walter had long disliked his name. Descended from the German word for "a mighty warrior," the name Walter did not fit Walter's perception of himself as a peacemaker. His surname, Hochstetler, meant "dweller on the hill," referring to the powerful Swiss-Germans who built their homes on the highest elevation of feudal towns. That name also did not seem like a good reflection of his personality.

In his seminary studies, Walter had discovered the richness of the name Michael. In Hebrew, the name Michael was a question: Who is like unto God? From the whole of Scripture, Walter believed that the answer to that question was "the man of peace." Michael also was the name of the guardian angel of the people of Israel. Michael was an advocate for the poor and the oppressed, a champion of justice.

But if Michael was to be Walter's new first name, what about his last name? At the time, he was reading "The Covenant of Peace" by Maurice Friedman, an exciting booklet about God's covenant of peace with his people. Friedman stated that he was grateful that his name meant "man of peace."

That was the clincher. Friedman, man of peace, also answered the question, "Who is like unto God?" Utilizing the spelling of his Germanic heritage, Walter Hochstetler took Michael Friedmann as his new name to signify his new identity.

The old Walter Hochstetler was a passive, nonresistant Amish boy. The new Michael Friedmann was an active peacemaker, vigorously working to usher in a new age of peace. Michael Friedmann was a member of the exciting draft resistance movement. He had visions of being a part of a groundswell of resisters, people who would symbolize the future of an America where all the people would stand up and say no to a militaristic government.

Michael began to turn his energies toward working more directly with the Mennonite draft resistance movement. He wrote articles for the Mennonite Draft Resisters newsletter, talked to youth groups, and led workshops at meetings where the draft and the war were being discussed. He got involved in a few more public demonstrations protesting the war and volunteered at a draft counseling center in Elkhart.

Often in his writing and speaking, he made reference to the sixteenth-century Anabaptists as the Mennonite precedent for radical Christian discipleship. Michael saw the witness of draft resistance to be consistent with the early Anabaptist movement. Harold S. Bender, in his classic work, "The Anabaptist Vision," listed love, discipleship, and voluntary committed church membership as some of the core elements of the vision. All of these things were very important to Michael. In his continued involvement with the Fellowship of Hope, he attempted to live them out in daily practice. He heard nothing more from the draft board.

In the next few years he held a variety of part-time jobs. He also traveled to churches with a Mennonite Central Committee Peace Section team of peace teachers, and attended a peace education seminar at Earlham School of Religion in Indiana.

The Fellowship of Hope continued to be the church and religious community that guided him. In 1973 the community employed him to do a variety of tasks—write dramas, visit students on the Goshen College campus, be a liaison with other house churches in Goshen, and work with Shalom Publishers, a mail-order center which he had set up to distribute literature about peace issues, Christian community, and church renewal. In 1974 Michael married Frances Zerger. They have since continued to live at the Fellowship of Hope.

Over the years he has refused to pay war taxes to the Internal Revenue Service because he wants to contribute neither his money nor his body to violent activity. In 1979 Michael participated in a demonstration in Washington, D.C., where he, along with a few others, poured blood on the steps of the Pentagon to protest the nuclear arms race and increasing militarism of the American government. He was arrested and detained briefly in prison.

His draft resistance experience has been an ongoing influence in his life. When he first returned his draft card, he felt an invigorating sense of freedom. Freedom to obey God, to take radical action, to respond without fear of the consequences. His commitment to work for social justice was heightened through his resistance. While he has been employed as a caseworker for the county welfare program since 1974, he hopes in the future to devote more time to peace education tasks, and to work more directly with the needs of local poor people, to help bring about justice and peace in their lives.

Michael has undergone yet another name change. In the spring of 1980 he attended a charismatic Christian retreat that focused on the healing of memories. He felt the Lord was telling him that God loved both parts of him: the quiet, sheltered Amish boy, and the active, peacemaking draft resister. He felt God's Spirit telling him that he should also accept both parts of himself. With that acceptance came a love for himself and his parents, and a decision to once again use the name Walter Hochstetler.

Becoming "Walter" again felt like coming full circle, back to who he was in the beginning. His years as Michael had been helpful in developing other facets of himself. Now, as he reassumed the name Walter, his desire to be an obedient disciple of the Prince of Peace felt more whole.

9.

Step Forth and Say Gently, "This Cannot Be"

David Rensberger

David Rensberger lives in Atlanta, Georgia, with his wife, Sharon Bottomley Rensberger, and their two daughters. He teaches New Testament at the Interdenominational Theological Center, a predominately black seminary in Atlanta.

When i said no
  to Selective Service
  i wasn't sure i was right
  i could not justify myself
  i only dimly perceived

                                    the wrong of it

  just knew
  i wasn't doing what they asked
  no matter what
They sent me forms
i sent them poems
  what i did was wrong
  i skeetered on the edge of standing up
and so i did not
stand up
Until
on seeing someone else's courage
  i did act
  and (for once) had a few reasons
  embryonic as they were
  for doing it
To return a draft card
  is nothing
To know why you did it is more
To ignore an order to report
  is nothing
To be convinced that it was right to do so

                                    is everything

And to know why it was right is even more
But the action came first

                                    and it was right*

_____

*Excerpted from Dave Rensberger's letter from prison to delegates at a 1971
conference of the Mennonite General Conference churches, meeting in Fresno,
California.

Dave Rensberger mailed back his draft cards in December 1969 because he knew he had to. It felt like it was the right thing to do.

He could not find an elaborate intellectual justification for returning his cards. He was simply convinced that God did not want him to heed the call of the Selective Service System. He acted as he felt God leading him to act. And later, the reasons why he should not cooperate with the draft became more and more clear as he followed a path of increasing resistance.

For the past year, Dave had been living as a hippie in hippie country—the hills of New Mexico. In the late 1960s, they were a tranquil haven for thousands of young Americans who wanted to get away from it all, not just for a weekend but forever.

The skies were the deepest of blues there; the snows the whitest of whites. Color-strewn mountains swooped up and down and back and forth between one's eyes and the horizon. The steep hillsides each had their own incredible hues, glowing brilliantly as the sun lay on them before nightfall.

He would take long walks whenever he felt like it, often with Sharon, his common-law wife. The two of them had lived for a time in a tiny cabin perched on the side of a canyon that dropped off sharply below them. The road led right up to their door and stopped, just as if Dave and Sharon lived at the end of one world and the beginning of another.

Sharon had written back to a bank in Indiana to close out her savings account to pay six months of rent on the place. They bought a small stockpile of staple goods and retreated. Life together was all they needed. They could just about get all of their earthly possessions on their backs. Sharon sewed and quilted and read. Dave read St. Paul's writings, the Gospels, and the complete works of Shakespeare in between tilling their vegetable garden. They would play with some puppy dogs and talk to each other all day, quietly, warmly. Dave and Sharon's love was strong and deep, welding them ever more tightly together as each day passed.

Then the post office began to catch up with them. His folks found out where they were. Letters went back and forth fairly regularly after that. One day the draft board's letters began getting to their post office box too. Mr. David Rensberger was supposed to report for his physical and go to work in alternative service in an Indianapolis hospital.

Dave knew from the start that he would not go. There probably were some principles lurking behind his "no," but at that point he was not acting out of a distinct philosophy of resistance. He just could not follow their orders because he had long before "dropped out." He and Sharon were participants in building a new life in a new kingdom. They had left the old society for good—let the dead bury the dead. Their alternative culture had nothing to do with warring. They served God rather than mammon. They shared instead of hoarded. They loved each other, eschewing competition and strife. They were gentle, not hostile. They enjoyed a peace that abolished anxiety. They lived in tune with and close to nature, abhoring the concrete and steel of the city.

The draft board was trying to force him back into straight society. But that would be the exact opposite of what they had decided their life was to be about.

Dave answered the induction notice with a letter telling the draft board members he had taken too many drugs to be any good for them. He hoped his detailed descriptions and exaggerations would scare them off. They didn't. The draft board's next letter he answered in a crazy, rambling fashion and tied the pages together with bright colored lengths of yarn. He was being honest with them: he was a hippie and they were on a draft board, and the two of them had nothing in common. Undaunted, they kept writing back.

Dave was near his wit's end. He told the draft board in Indiana that there just was no way he could afford to travel to Indiana to get his physical. It provided a bit of a delay but they were soon nipping at his heels again, ordering him to report for a physical in New Mexico. To gain some more time, and to live closer to some friends of theirs, Dave and Sharon moved to Taos, New Mexico.

J ust as the draft board letters began to catch up with them again, the publishers of *The Mennonite,* an official magazine of the General Conference Mennonite Church, caught up with their address changes too. Dave began to read news in *The Mennonite* of young Mennonites who were resisting the draft, refusing either to register or to do alternative service because they said they could not in conscience cooperate with the conscription system in any way. Finally, reading a letter from one resister in the December 16, 1969, issue, Dave came to a definite decision. He felt deeply that God had led Sharon and him to New Mexico, and that God was definitely not leading them anywhere else, at least not for the time being. The state was calling, God was calling, and Dave decided he would heed his God. He got an envelope, put his draft cards inside, and mailed them back to the draft board. In a note, he explained that he was severing his relationship with the draft board because his conscience would not allow him to cooperate with the Selective Service System any longer.

By then Dave and Sharon were living in a commune with some people they had known from earlier "drop-out" days.

These people were not into antiwar demonstrations. Their opposition to the war was expressed in their building an alternative society, inaugurating a new world and a new way to live. They saw their life as a refuge from the other world. Secluded as they were, Dave was sure the FBI would never find him. No one in the area seemed particularly fond of the federal government.

Meanwhile, a healthy baby girl was born to Dave and Sharon in March 1970. They named her Felicity; she was their pride and joy. Having a child expressed their hope in the future. The new alternative life they were building was not just for themselves, it was for Felicity and her generation.

But other generations have a claim on children too. In August Dave and Sharon hitched a ride to their homes in northern Indiana. They wanted the grandparents to see their firstborn grandchild.

Their arrival caused a stir. Dave and Sharon were notorious, local kids who two years before had run away from a complacent rural community to join a frightening crowd of "rebellious hippies" who were rejecting all the values of normal American society.

Yet Dave and Sharon were difficult to peg. They did not fit the stereotype of wild, hostile prophets angrily denouncing mainstream society. They lived out their views quietly and peacefully. Dave was such a warm and gentle man that people could not stay upset with him for long. Sharon and Dave obviously had a permanent, solid love and loyalty for each other. Their child was adorable. Most puzzling was their reverent spirituality. One could see that they had a vibrant and meaningful relationship with the Lord Jesus Christ. Yet they were not living like normal Christians.

Actually, they were not normal Christians. The more Dave's mother, Lois Rensberger, got to know the two of them again, now grown-ups returned to her home, the more she thought of them as first-century Christians. They had changed since they'd left home.

Dave had been through a lot. His usual disposition, from childhood on up, was to take things as they came. He was never a crusader. He tended to try to go with the flow, to fit in, to not stand apart. But because of his scholastic ability, he had always stuck out. To compensate for this when he was a child, Dave tried to make everything else about himself be normal. When clothes shopping with his mother, he would pick muted colors and quiet tones. Dave was a very little guy compared to his school buddies, and they nicknamed him "Herc" for Hercules, the Greek god of strength and brawn. He had started school early, at age five; his classmates started at age seven or eight. At the small grade school he attended, most of the students were Amish. Boys were not supposed to enjoy studying, only girls were. But classwork was his forte, and he couldn't help liking it.

Books became young Dave's consuming passion, gathering knowledge a habit. Once the entire family was watching a basketball championship on television—all of them, that is, except Dave. He was lying with the other children on the floor, but he was engrossed in an encyclopedia, oblivious to their excitement. When someone asked Dave what in the world he was doing, he blithely replied that he had started to look up the Emancipation Proclamation but had gotten sidetracked.

Young Dave became even younger among his peers when he skipped grade five. By the time high school rolled around, his friends were all driving and dating. But Dave had to be driven to the high school prom by his parents. After editing the high school student newspaper, Dave graduated at age sixteen and entered Indiana's Purdue University three months later. It was a natural place to go to college. His father, Melvin Rensberger, had graduated there.

Purdue was at once traumatic and enjoyable for Dave. In the end, it offered him the possibility to do what he still calls one of his most original acts.

At age eighteen, after two years of college life, he dropped out of sight without a trace. That brash act, along with returning his draft cards later, broke his usual tendency to just fit in, conform, not stick out.

Dave had floundered at first at Purdue, overwhelmed by the advanced courses he immediately took because of his prodigy status as a National Merit Scholarship honor recipient. Plus it was his first time away from home and rural life. He failed a course that semester; he had never before received a grade lower than an "A." Dave soon shifted his major from math to creative writing and began to feel more at ease.

He had some very good times after the initial problems. Those years, 1965 and 1966, were before the main wave of campus antiwar protests, but Purdue's few activists did hold several demonstrations for civil rights. Once, the campus "hippies" (Dave and a handful of others) organized an event they called "Gentle Thursday." They handed out little gifts to students on a beautiful spring day, trying to communicate that there were things in life worth living for besides engineering, animal husbandry, or the technical sciences.

December 1966 was Dave's eighteenth birthday and he registered for the draft, filed a statement as a Mennonite conscientious objector, and received a student deferment. The Vietnam War was only beginning to be a matter of public concern and controversy. With his Mennonite background, he simply knew he was opposed to any form of warfare; it was a sin and a crime.

His good experiences at Purdue were dampened by some late-adolescent confusion, however. He had a growing sense of not being able to find his "place in the cosmos." It just seemed that he was not accomplishing anything important in school. So at the end of his second year at Purdue, in May 1967, when his mother drove to Lafayette to pick him up, Dave was nowhere to be found. He had disappeared without telling his family where he was going.

He asked a close friend to mail a letter to his parents a few days later from somewhere in the East. In it Dave vaguely indicated that he was heading for New York City. It was a deliberate deception, covering his tracks. Actually, he was heading due west for the Haight-Ashbury district of San Francisco.

Life magazine had pictured Haight-Ashbury as the mecca of tomorrow's flower children of peace and love. Dave was fascinated by the stories of communes and people living in a life of love and togetherness that contrasted with the materialism and strife of mainstream society. In a sense, Dave really was not running away; he was running toward something that sounded terrific. He hitchhiked, reached the coast in three or four days, and assumed another name. He was starting his life anew. How exhilarating it was! Dave did not contact his parents for months.

Meanwhile, the Rensbergers' pastor, Jacob Mireau, met with Melvin and Lois, trying to ease their fear and pain. The very day Lois had gone to Purdue to pick up her son, the Lafayette daily newspaper had printed a letter to the editor from Dave that spoke out against a recent speech by a visiting dignitary who advocated racial segregation. It was an ironic symbol of how painful their pride in their son had become. He was so gifted, and now so messed up. Mislead by Dave's letter, they made futile attempts to reach him at a commune they had heard about in New York City.

The Rensbergers' fears were compounded by their

knowledge that Dave was experimenting with drugs. At that time many people considered drug use to be virtually suicidal. Pot smoking especially was thought to turn kids into lifelong vegetables. The Rensbergers changed their family will to provide "permanent institutional care" for Dave if needed.

W hen he arrived in San Francisco, Dave knew no one. He had no place to stay, but then neither did hundreds of other young people. They would all just crash one night here or one night there, in a hallway or someone's apartment. Dave met all sorts of people in the park, at Tracey's donut shop on Haight Street, and on the sidewalks. The money he brought along ran out quickly though; he tried to panhandle, but discovered he simply was not good at it.

Then one morning Dave ran across a group headed for a commune farm called Morningstar, north of the city. He jumped on the back of their pickup truck, and ended up staying at Morningstar for more than a year. By the end of his first summer at Morningstar, he got back in touch with his parents and let them know he was okay.

Morningstar was a patch of land on which a couple dozen people had settled around a man named Lou Gottlieb. Lou had been a rather famous folk singer with a group called "The Limeliters" before he had dropped out of Hollywood entertainment and bought the Morningstar land. Lou had decided it was not for him to say who should come or go; the land was God's and the place was God's and people had a God-given right to use it as they pleased. He believed that individual ownership and management of property was at the root of society's ills, and eventually succeeded in getting legal title transferred from his name over to God's.

It was impossible for Dave to feel out of place at Morningstar. Everyone belonged. It was an indescribably pleasant, relaxed setting. People simply hung out all day, reading the masterpieces of the ancient mystics, philosophers, and religious writers, making beautiful music, taking mind-expanding drugs, growing a few vegetables, and living amicably with one another. Dave could use his mind for fun, he did not have to produce scholastically. He was fitting into a group that was very different from the rest of society and yet he felt perfectly fine about it. He had found his people.

Dave began to be drawn to the Scriptures. Amazed, he discovered that St. Paul's writings on nonconformity to the world in a sense fit with what Morningstar was about. Dave followed Jesus' teachings on taking no thought for the morrow very seriously—every day. The Sermon on the Mount, the Gospels, the account of the acts of the early church, all began to take on expanded meaning for him. His "place in the cosmos" began to become clear; a deeper relationship with Jesus and God mystically grew within him. He had many rich, deep periods of reflection there.

Dave went home for a visit the following summer. He wanted to see the folks again, but he had no intention of staying very long. He also looked up Sharon Bottomley, a friend from high school. They had worked together on the school newspaper and had written back and forth while he was at Purdue. A few days after Dave left home to return to Morningstar with little more than a new copy of the New Testament and a new pair of socks, Sharon wrote a note to her parents and caught a plane to San Francisco to join Dave. About one month later, in the fall of 1968, they moved to idyllic New Mexico. They both wanted to get away from the beck and call of their parents for a while.

The two years in New Mexico cemented their relationship as well as their Christian faith. When Dave returned to Indiana in 1970, he was strong in himself and God. He was ready to be closer to more orthodox Christians, to speak with their terminology, but on a different, more radical scale.

Dave, Sharon, and Felicity lived with Dave's folks during the entire fall of 1970. For Dave and Sharon, his resistance was one of the last things on their minds over this period; the draft board had not written to him in months.

One day, the FBI came on one of its usual rounds to ask the Rensbergers for Dave's latest address. Sharon answered the doorbell.

"Hello, is David Rensberger here?" the agent asked, expecting a negative answer. "Oh, you must be his sister."

"No, I'm his wife," replied Sharon. The agent's eyes lit up brightly as she continued unawares. "Dave'll be back soon, he's just out picking up some hogs with his dad."

"Well, we'll be back soon too," said the agent, and drove away. When Dave heard about the visit later that day, he went down to the FBI office. He briefly explained his reasons for resisting, that he was prepared to go through with any court proceedings, and that he wanted to take a short trip to see some of his friends in New Mexico before his arrest. He meant it when he said he would return, but they did not believe him and speeded up their plans to arrest him.

On a midweek morning a few days later, Dave and Sharon were in the living room listening to Simon and Garfunkel's album "Bridge over Troubled Waters" when the doorbell rang. Outside were a couple of beefy marshals ready to arrest Dave. Dave and Sharon were given a few minutes to get Dave's things together. The arrest was more sudden than they had expected. Alone, they held each other and prayed.

His parents borrowed several thousand dollars against the farm and were able to bail him out later that day. While he waited for his trial, Dave's case became the topic of lively discussion in northern Indiana. At about the same time, a Church of the Brethren member in the area, Darrell Weybright, had refused to register after his eighteenth birthday and his case stirred up community debate too. One day, the entire editorial page of *The Goshen News* was taken up by letters, pro and con, on their draft resistance. One was from a 90-year-old man who articulately supported what Dave was doing. This and other letters meant a lot to Dave.

Dave wrote several articles during this time for *The Mennonite, Gospel Herald,* and *Christian Living,* all Mennonite church periodicals. His mother also wrote several articles defending draft resistance and describing her feelings as the mother of a young man who was being prosecuted by the government for his beliefs.

The gist of Dave's writings was that the government had no right to order people to serve, only God could do that. While some other guys may honestly feel simultaneously called by God and the state to serve at the same place, Dave wrote that he had been called by God to build "a different lifestyle, an alternative society, so that my children may never know war and conscription." The state's call was in conflict with that vision because institutionalized alternative service would mean he could not follow God's specific call for him. His approach had a unique twist. Many of the other Mennonite resistance arguments focused more on nonparticipation in the military system, or on the need to loudly oppose the militaristic aims of surrounding society. Dave was not in personal contact with any other young Mennonites who were resisting nor did he see much literature on the subject. He simply zeroed in on Scripture, taking at face value passages like Peter's vow to "obey God rather than man."

Formulating reasons for his draft resistance was not easy for Dave. Over the past four years he had not been used to thinking things through under pressure. His logic may have been somewhat out of practice, his reasoning a bit weak at points. But he plowed ahead because he knew what he was doing was right; the reasons would become clearer in the end, he believed. In many ways, though they were now in straight society, Dave and Sharon's minds were still in laid-back New Mexico.

Between the November 1970 arrest and April 1971 trial, Dave and Sharon continued to be actively involved in church life at the Silver Street congregation, a small rural General Conference Mennonite church near Middlebury, Indiana. People seemed to accept them after the initial shock. More than anything else, the members there were troubled by Dave and Sharon's officially unmarried state, but that soon receded as they began to see how committed Dave and Sharon were to each other. Later, they did get formally married by their pastor, in part to heed Paul's advice to avoid needlessly offending one's fellow church members.

Dave and Sharon also regularly attended an interfaith, charismatic fellowship that met weekly in Goshen, and met several times with a Christian community in Elkhart called Fellowship of Hope, which they considered joining. But the legal proceedings were soon upon them and they began to lose control over their lives at the hands of the government.

Dave's sentencing was set for the morning of Good Friday in 1971. He had earlier pleaded guilty, preparing no defense. As far as he was concerned, there was no point in going through with a trial. They should just sentence him and get on with it. Darrell Weybright had just been sentenced before him to three years in prison, the area judge's normal penalty for draft resisters. But Dave did not fear jail, he believed God would see him through.

Walking into the courtroom that morning, Dave was struck by the architecture of the court building. It was a temple to a pagan religion, Dave thought, looking at the high ceilings, somber wood paneling and general hush and plush of the place. There were even church-like benches in the courtroom, a wide open space between the audience and the judge's raised dais, and everyone was obliged to stand up when the judge entered.

The courtroom was packed that morning with Dave's supporters from the Silver Street congregation, the charismatic fellowship, and the Mennonite seminary in Elkhart. Before the session began, J. C. Wenger, noted Mennonite church historian, author, and preacher, showed Dave a copy of a letter he had sent to the judge. It said that about 2,000 years before, another innocent man was condemned for his righteousness on Good Friday, and that Wenger hoped that history would not be repeated in this courtroom.

Before Dave was sentenced he had a chance to make a statement. He repeated what for him had become the primary reason for his refusal to obey Selective Service orders: God had not called him to an officially approved form of service. God had a different kind of work for him and he had to obey God rather than Caesar.

". . . There does come a time when these human institutions, made up as they are of men prone to error like anybody else, may step out of their place. . . . And when this happens, it is up to individuals, whose consciences seek God, to step forth and say, in a spirit of gentleness, this is not so. And for this reason we are willing to make sacrifices, if necessary. . . ."

The judge, obviously exasperated by a young person who was not open to following the law for the law's sake, erupted at the end with the charge that he found Dave "dangerous to society." "If a man is to decide which law he shall obey and which he shall disrespect, our system of government under laws has been torn asunder," he said, rapping his gavel and pronouncing the sentence: three years in the Federal Corrections Institution at Ashland, Kentucky. Dave was allowed to spend the Easter weekend at home before he was jailed Monday morning.

P rison. It changed his life. He hurt deeply because of it. He learned some crucial lessons. He made decisions that determined the direction of his future life. He also had some very enjoyable moments. But prison was prison. It locked him up, barred from society, controlled, dehumanized. Most agonizing was the separation from his wife and daughter.

Once as Sharon and Felicity were sitting with Dave in the austere, plastic visiting lounge, two-year-old Felicity pulled Dave's clothes locker key out of his pocket, purposefully tottered over to the locked door leading to the outside, and stuck the key in the keyhole, trying to unlock the door to let her daddy out so he could go home with mommy and her. Dave found it excruciating to explain to Felicity that, while he really wanted to go home with her, the prison would not let him. His key could not free him. It was impossible for a little girl to understand.

Visiting hours were on Saturdays, Sundays, and Wednesdays; Sharon and Felicity had moved to Ashland so they could come visit each day. If the weather was nice, they were allowed to sit outside where they could eat picnic lunches Sharon prepared, a welcome relief from Dave's monotonous prison food. On the nights before visiting days, Sharon would hoist Felicity up on the kitchen counter to help make the lunches. She would talk a lot about Dave to Felicity, trying to compensate for the short time daddy and daughter had together each week.

On bad weather days Sharon and Dave would sit close together all day in the visitors' lounge, reading stories to Felicity, playing with her and her toys. Sharon and Dave tried to keep up with each other's thoughts. Sometimes having nothing to say, they sat together quietly, Sharon knitting and Dave playing with Felicity.

In a way Sharon and Felicity were as imprisoned as Dave. Visiting him inside prison, they were controlled just like prisoners. Outside they were separated from the main person in their lives—Dave. Prison even kept Felicity in diapers much longer than she might otherwise have been. She would announce that she must "go potty" but it would take the guards an average of 10 minutes to heed her parents' pleas and open the bathroom. Such a delayed response can wreck the best of toilet training patterns.

On days between visits Dave would write to Sharon and Felicity. He would enclose a special letter for Felicity, but pretty soon his imagination began to run out of things to write. So he took to tracing animals onto paper, spelling the animal's name in big letters, and writing a small description about what color the animal was, what it ate, and so forth. Sharon would read the animal letters to Felicity, who enjoyed them very much.

Dave was concerned about how little contact he had with his daughter. He wrote a poem about the future when he would be free and Felicity would be a big girl. It said that if he did not pay much attention to her then, she should remind him about the time when they did not get to kiss each other every night.

As Dave's term stretched out, he gradually climbed the "good behavior" ladder inside the prison. Ashland was a prison for young offenders, a minimum security institution. When each inmate first arrived, however, he was placed in the tightest security section with the most restrictions. After awhile, if there

were no "incidents," and if the prisoner was generally cooperative, he would advance to medium security, and finally,
minimum security.

Good behavior also allowed inmates to have more
private, less disciplined living quarters, and provided an op-
tional, once-a-month "town trip" in which the inmate was
allowed out of prison for a twelve-hour period to visit family
and friends within a few miles of the jail. One could save up two
months' visits and take two twelve-hour day trips in a row. The
main requirement was that one of the inmate's parents had to
sign him out and be responsible to bring him back on time each
evening. One did not take any chances on town trips; the liberty
would be lifted immediately if caught breaking any rules.

Dave was able to go on all the town trips he was allowed,
with his parents driving the eight hours each time to sign him
out. They would eat or go to church together, and then the
grandparents would take Felicity off on a little jaunt, leaving
Dave and Sharon a short time to be alone. Felicity, thinking
grandma and grandpa came down just to see her, was always
delighted. But it was very difficult for her to understand why her
daddy had to leave the apartment to go back to prison each
evening. At least once she was in tears, wailing, "Daddy, don't
go. Daddy, don't go 'way."

The entire family spent the first Christmas together in
Sharon's apartment. Dave's grandparents, parents, two
brothers, and his sister drove all day to get there. But of course
the holiday mood was broken abruptly by early evening when
Dave had to go back to the jail.

Returning to the prison after a town trip was always painful. Dave had to take off his "town clothes," bend over and be
strip searched (some of the guards seemed to take perverse delight in probing his naked body), put on the all-tan prison uniform, and walk back into the life of controls and bars and rigid

schedules, locked away from his family. It seemed unreal, like he was living in a movie. He was Dave Rensberger, husband, daddy. Then he was David Rensberger, inmate number 18676. Back and forth.

D ave's fellow inmates were an odd assortment of people, many of them just kids. The blacks were mainly from Northern cities, in on larceny charges. Most of the whites were rural Southerners, sentenced for car theft or general robbery. All of them were petty criminals, often first-time offenders. People inside prison were really about the same as those outside, Dave found. They were just more tightly packed together and thus more readily irritated.

Racial tension sometimes erupted. One particular time, the film *Gone with the Wind* was shown in two parts on two consecutive nights. The blacks did not like the racially prejudiced portrayal of their race. The whites tended to think that portrayal was correct. By the second evening the mood was volatile and things would have come to violent blows except for the fact that, for Dave, a villain even greater than racial bigotry entered: male sexism. When Butler slapped Scarlett in the movie, the black and white male audience cheered. Dave was horrified by how it brought everyone together. Here were inmates, being treated like nonpersons, who turned right around and treated women like nonpersons. This and other experiences made him an ardent feminist before his release.

Prison changed him in many other ways, not the least of which was that his faith deepened. The first night he was jailed, the bunk he was randomly assigned to had the letters Y-H-W-H scratched into the ceiling above it. He took it as a sign of Yahweh—God's presence with him. The next night, in a different cell, his new bunk again held a sign: a cross etched with detailed care into the wall, radiant beams emanating out from its center. This symbol of Christ's suffering was profoundly comforting to Dave. It confirmed what he already knew, Christ was going to be close to him in this ordeal.

Dave tried to live out his nonviolent beliefs in his relationships with other inmates. A few times this proved difficult. He was not often seriously threatened with physical harm, but one time a mixed-up, seventeen-year-old bully physically harassed Dave to try to get him to buy him some cigarettes or candy from his concession account. Dave attempted to respond from the gospel standpoint of giving to all who ask, not resisting even a violent demand. But he found it hard to love this "enemy." He gave in and bought the stuff out of fear. He guessed one had to be very close to Jesus to actually love an enemy. Other times he resisted, not to the point of punching, but he refused to give in. Before he entered prison, he had not thought much about how hard it might be to be a nonviolent person in a place that was run by violence and that evoked violence.

Because of his continuing good behavior and renewed academic orientation, Dave was able to enroll in "Newgate," the prison's education program which was designed to offer inmates a new entrance into society at the end of their term. He was a bit rusty, having been out of school for three years. But he studied passionately, taking, among other things, a course on child development. He was, after all, a father.

Lois, Dave's mother, had given him a *Westminster Dictionary of the Bible* when he entered prison. He spent long hours studying the Bible with the dictionary close at hand. One day he was delighted to discover that someone had placed an unusual book—a translation of one of the Dead Sea Scrolls—in the prison library. It helped shape his academic interests. Meanwhile, Jacob Enz, of the Associated Mennonite Biblical

Seminaries in Elkhart, kept in touch with Dave. Enz encouraged him in his biblical studies, and bought him a beginning membership in a scholarly society called the American Schools of Oriental Research.

Enz knew some people at Harvard University and told them about Dave's interest and situation. Paul Hanson, Harvard professor of Old Testament, collected a shipment of used books from his students at Harvard Divinity School and sent them to Dave in prison. They were a godsend. At about the same time, David Habegger, a Mennonite pastor in Elkhart who had been especially close to Dave and his mother, helped arrange for Dave to take a correspondence course in the Hebrew language from the University of Wisconsin. His parents helped pay for it.

There was a small circle of inmates at Ashland incarcerated on drug and draft charges. He met up with them on his first or second day at Ashland, when, in a discussion with a prison guard on the Vietnam war, Dave voiced a Christ-oriented comment about living in peace rather than war. A good number of the draft violators were there because of their religious beliefs, including Church of the Brethren, Quaker, and Jehovah's Witness faiths. Those jailed for drug violations often held the same antiwar viewpoints as those in on draft charges.

One of the most important measures of support from the outside was the visits of friends from churches and the peace movement. Sometimes visitors were allowed to arrange group meetings with the draft-charged inmates. The visits gave Dave and other draft-charged inmates a chance to talk with people who had similar peace interests, allowing them to keep up on news of the antiwar movement and chat about things they would talk about if they were outside.

Dave's reasons for resisting the draft broadened

somewhat while he was in prison. Before, his public arguments had centered on God's versus Caesar's right to conscript service. A half year into his jail term, he wrote a concise article for *Gospel Herald,* one of the Mennonite Church magazines, in which he focused, as a draft resister, on outlining some scriptural understandings of repentance, nonviolence, nationalism, and the church as a new kingdom that must resist the kingdoms of this world.

T he routine of prison life was so overbearing, so all-encompassing, that he tended to take delight in anything that broke the monotony. Ashland, Kentucky, often gets fogged in. On foggy mornings, the regular routine would be broken. The guards would not send the inmates to their work details because it would be too easy for prisoners to take off in the mist, climb the fence, and lose themselves into freedom. Dave has loved foggy days ever since.

Except for the strip searches, the thrice daily "count" was the most dehumanizing aspect of prison life. Around breakfast, supper, and bedtime, the same loudspeaker that urgently barked everyone awake each morning with a strident "Wake up, wake up," would bellow out to all corners of the prison, "Count, count." Immediately each prisoner had to line up and not move until the guards completed their walk-around count to make sure everyone was still there. The guards had a central tracking station and knew where everyone should be in a given moment. If the numbers did not match, they would make everyone stay where they were until they found out who was missing. They would even check the bathroom each time to count anyone who had been in there when the count had started. If a guy was sitting on a commode with the stall door closed, he was supposed to simply stay put during the count.

The guards would note his legs under the stall door and move on.

One day the count came out wrong. There was one person too many in Dave's block. Finally, after counting five separate times, the guards discovered what was wrong.

Some inmates, in a daring attempt to break the routine, frustrate the guards, and enjoy a delightful joke, had sneaked an extra pair of pants and shoes into the john, stuffed them with rolls of newspapers, locked the stall door from the inside, and crawled out over the top when no one was looking. Then they had waited with furtive glee as the guards searched high and low.

When the guards finally discovered the "phantom inmate of the head," they were quite upset. Obviously this ruse could have been used by an inmate to cover an escape, gaining hours on his pursuers. From then on, a rule was laid down that if an inmate was sitting in the john during count, he was to move his feet back and forth vigorously so the guards could tell he was for real.

By April of 1972, Dave had served one year of his three-year sentence. Normally, after anyone had served a third of his or her federal sentence, one's case would come up before a parole board for a possible early parole. But only very rarely was early parole granted at the one-third mark. Usually the case was set aside for a second review months later.

For early parole to be granted, one had to propose a parole plan that described where one would go and what one would do. Linked as he was with the University of Wisconsin through the Hebrew language correspondence courses he was taking, Dave applied to the university for admission for the fall 1972 semester and was accepted.

Eagerly Dave awaited the board's verdict on his parole. They finally approved it, but gave him a parole date that was three weeks later than the day he had to be on campus to register. He could not go to school if he could not get there in time to register, which meant he could not be paroled in the first place because he could not get into school, his approved parole assignment. It was the letdown of his life.

It was too much for Dave's mother. She called up her Indiana congressman, Representative John Brademas in Washington, D.C., explained the situation, and asked him to pull some strings. It worked. Brademas got the parole board to move up the date of Dave's release. If it had been up to just the Rensbergers, Brademas would have been reelected forever.

August 1972. The sun was coming up as Dave rolled out of Ashland on a Greyhound bus bound for Wisconsin. It was a daylong ride, just perfect for deep reflection on the quiet exhilaration he felt. A new life lay before him. Freedom at last, after sixteen long months.

Sharon met him at the Madison bus station. She had gone on ahead to find an apartment, and his folks had moved their stuff for them the week before. Their first couple weeks back together again were a huge adjustment for both of them. Sharon was accustomed to making all the decisions, having been the lone parent and head of household for the past sixteen months. But after being treated like a little child by the prison for the past sixteen months, Dave was anxious to be in charge. They weathered the difficulty, although not without feeling guilty, because freedom was not as immediately blissful as it was supposed to be.

F reedom was a shocking reality. Dave was thrilled by very little things, like being able to handle matches again, to carry keys that locked and secured his doors against everyone, to grow his hair and beard back to comfortable lengths, and to go where he wanted, within the confines of the parole officer's permission.

Dave and Sharon quickly found that their interests were focused almost exclusively on his academics, their church friends, and their growing daughter. They both quickly fit in with people at Geneva Chapel, a campus-based fellowship group of the Christian Reformed Church.

Dave majored in Hebrew and Semitic studies. In three years, he finished both his bachelor's and master's degrees. Then he went to Yale University as a graduate student in the Religious Studies department, gaining a doctoral degree in New Testament. While there, Miranda, their second daughter was born.

In the fall of 1980, he began his first professional job, teaching New Testament at the Interdenominational Theological Center, a seminary in Atlanta, Georgia. Having been only peripherally involved in social justice issues while in the world of academics, Dave said he and Sharon now hope to contribute their "time, energy, and thinking" to Christian groups that take "radical stands in opposition to the hatred, violence, injustice, and general ungodliness of the human race that most regard today as the normal way of life."

They felt closest to Christ back when Dave was in prison and times were lonely and difficult for both of them, when they were doing something that they were very convinced was the right thing to do. That closeness came from their struggles to follow the Lord. They had intensely tried to answer the question: Were they going to be part of the Vietnam War's solution, or part of the problem? They felt then, as now, that some people will respond to God's call one way, others will respond another way, and that it is important to preserve a variety of responses. But they were sure that God's purposes remain clear and unchanging.

"Mennonites," said Dave, "are well known as the quiet folks in the land. There is something very good and true about that. But when the land is filled with evil, then it is not necessarily good and faithful to remain quiet." He has not kept quiet in the past. His gentle spirit will naturally compel him to action in the future.

10.

Religious Convictions Aren't Nice to Have

Bruce A. Yoder

Bruce A. Yoder lives in Richmond, Virginia, and is the pastor of First Mennonite Church of Richmond.

B ruce was ready to resist the draft. The last hurdle had been crossed in talking it over with some very plain, conservative Mennonites he had just met. What they said and didn't say about draft resistance proved to be crucial. He valued discussing his ideas with people who approached life from a different angle.

He had spent much of the fall of 1969 talking with friends at Eastern Mennonite College (EMC) about the draft. Late-night bull sessions and cafeteria conversations often focused on what was a Christian individual's responsibility for the Vietnam War. One friend, Duane Shank, had refused to register. Others were considering returning their cards.

Bruce had registered for the draft a while back. Now he wanted to resist by returning his draft cards. His chief reason for resisting was the inequity of the selection process. While Mennonites could easily obtain permission to do alternative service, conscientious objectors who were not from a historic peace church background had a difficult time receiving the same exemption from military duty.

Even worse, non-Mennonite guys in his home area of Fulton County, Ohio, faced a greater chance of induction because the local draft boards had to fill their quota of young men to the military. Draft boards that handed out deferments and waivers, to Mennonites, for example, still had to draft a set number of soldiers each month. The more Mennonites in a community, the greater the likelihood that a non-Mennonite would be sent off to war.

It was unfair; it was that simple. Bruce decided he did not want to participate in such an injustice.

From his parents, John and Doris, he had gained a basic sense that one should always do what was right before God. But discerning exactly what was right was a different matter. His parents did not agree that it was necessary for him to resist the draft in order to do what was right, but they would not stand in the way of him following his conscience. He had talked with them at Thanksgiving, so he knew their views.

Bruce's home church, Central Mennonite in Archbold, Ohio, never played a critical role in his decision. It was a large church with more than 600 members, and he did not feel very close to the people there. Bruce had joined in a bit of correspondence with the pastor, Charles Gautsche, while he was at EMC. And Charles indicated that he felt Bruce was doing the wrong thing. The influence that folks back home had on this matter was really quite minimal.

During that same Thanksgiving break he had a hearing with his draft board. It was the culmination of a series of exchanges they had had with him by mail, in which he told them he was considering resisting and they warned him that it was illegal, advising him to reconsider.

Reconsidering, for him, meant talking with more people. It was then that he decided to discuss it with some of the very plain, conservative, Old Order Mennonites. He decided that if they agreed that draft resistance was valid, he would return his draft card. The opportunity to talk with a few of them came during Christmas break, when he joined some Old Order Mennonites on a Mennonite Disaster Service team in Mississippi, cleaning up after a hurricane.

Their response surprised him. Of all the people outside his tight circle of friends at EMC, they were the most supportive. "If your conscience tells you to resist, then go ahead and do it," was their simple advice. At that point he knew that he would return his draft cards.

The Mennonite Disaster Service crew was working close

enough to New Orleans so that he was able to visit the city one afternoon. As he strolled down a street by himself in the commercial district, he came upon a jewelry store named Shop of the Magi. Very appropriate, he thought, because of the Christmas season. He entered and began looking at the glittering jewelry. One ring caught his attention. It was rather wide, all silver, with the Greek letters "chi" and "rho" on it, the first two letters of the Greek word for Christ. He decided to purchase the ring and wear it as a symbol of Jesus being Lord of his life.

Being in that kind of relationship with Jesus meant taking steps of obedience, sometimes visible, sometimes invisible. He considered returning his draft cards a relatively minor, yet necessary, act of obedience.

He sent the cards back to Selective Service in January 1970 with a letter explaining his reasons. An annoying exchange of correspondence followed. In cool, detached, form-letter fashion, the Selective Service employees returned his card. And he, replying with another letter, again enclosed his draft cards in the envelope.

Once he allowed some of his humor to slip into a reply. Writing as if to a mail-order book club, Bruce indicated he no longer wanted to be a member of the organization and that he had given notice of his withdrawal on such and such a date, so would the club please remove his name from its list at once.

I n the spring of 1970, the government instituted a new means of choosing draftees. Bruce listened to the lottery drawing on the radio in his room at EMC. Several of his buddies who were interested in draft resistance were with him. The lottery, conducted by ranking birthdates in random order, gave Bruce a high number. The higher the number, the less chance of being drafted.

Bruce did not feel relieved when his birthdate fell in the safe range, nor did he think that his action had been useless. He had given little consideration to the consequences of his resistance. While he wondered what action his draft board might still take, he was well aware that people generally were not imprisoned for failing to carry their draft cards. The heavier sentences were levied on those who had not registered or who had refused induction. He had never feared jail because he had not seen it as a likely punishment in his case. Thoughts about the consequences occupied little of his time; he simply responded in a manner which he felt necessary as he attempted to follow Christ.

His concern for peace did not diminish after the lottery eliminated him from the draft. In May of 1970, four students were shot to death by National Guardsmen at Kent State University in Ohio. Bruce, along with thousands of students across the United States, felt a deep grief and shock at this senseless tragedy. He and a few other students at EMC looked for a way to respond. Final exams were scheduled to begin at EMC a few days after the killings occurred. They decided that to participate in the finals would be going on with business as usual and that the circumstances required something more drastic than business as usual. They talked it over with their professors and refused to take their finals, instead spending their time discussing the shootings with local businessmen.

Talking with the businessmen was both frightening and fascinating. Many felt that the shootings were justifiable, even necessary. Some even refused to talk about it. Nevertheless, the students still felt that their effort to boycott exams had been worthwhile. Having the faculty dock their marks one letter grade did not seem too severe, although some students' positions on the dean's list were jeopardized.

The most personally difficult event at EMC for Bruce

came when he lost his bid for reelection as president of the
Student Government Association. In his first term of office, he
had lobbied the administration to allow students to take more
responsibility for their lives on EMC's campus. Bruce had previously attended Ball State, a large Indiana university, and
many of EMC's regulations, like the 11:00 p.m. dorm curfew,
seemed petty and adolescent. He wanted EMC's administration to treat students like they were adults. In his reelection
campaign, Bruce's style of working with the administration became an issue. Bruce was perceived as being anti-administra-
tion and anti-establishment. He lost the election by a landslide,
with the students voting two to one for Bruce's opponent. It
deeply hurt him.

The summer of 1970 helped ease some of Bruce's painful
feelings. He worked as a summer recreation director
under Mennonite Central Committee with a Methodist church
in Nashville, Tennessee. The church's pastor, Bill Barnes, supported him in his draft resistance.

Another helpful friend was Judy Parks, a woman he got to
know that summer. She accepted him, he felt, in a way no one
else ever had before; with her he began to see and understand
new parts of himself. She also helped to cast a new light on his
draft resistance. Returning his draft card had been a personal,
necessary statement. He had seen inequity and he had
responded. Like a poem, his draft resistance had welled up inside and pushed its way outward.

Toward the end of the summer, at a national Mennonite
youth convention, Bruce led a workshop on draft resistance.
He liked keeping in contact with the younger kids, helping
them to sort out their responses to militarism while being careful not to tell them what to do. He believed draft resistance had

to be a personal, carefully thought-out decision.

Bruce returned to EMC in the fall. He had not heard anything from the Selective Service for quite some time. Then one day as he was eating lunch, the cafeteria manager came up to him, saying that he had a phone call for Bruce from an FBI agent.

When Bruce picked up the phone, the agent told him that he was on campus and would like to talk with him.

"Okay," replied Bruce. "Why don't you join me for lunch?"

"No, I want to talk with you alone," said the agent. "I'm in the dean of students' office."

"I'll be with you as soon as I finish my lunch," Bruce responded.

When he stepped outside a bit later, he noticed that the weather had turned strange while he was eating. A freak show of thunder and lightning was accompanying a snowstorm. Walking the short distance to the administration building, dark clouds swirling overhead, his uneasiness grew. He didn't know what to expect.

He felt some anger toward EMC. It seemed the college was making it so easy for the FBI, giving an agent a room right there on campus. What was worse, the administration did not give any warning or any other visible sign of support to Bruce. They just turned the phone over to the FBI guy and looked the other way.

The agent who was waiting for him appeared fairly young, maybe 35. His well-trimmed, neatly combed hair, and his gray suit with matching briefcase, gave him a banker's appearance. He handled the interview in a businesslike manner, first wanting Bruce to explain to him why he had returned his draft cards. Bruce repeated his reasons, describing the religious motivations that he had written about to the draft board.

The agent quickly dismissed Bruce's answers, saying, "The government gives you guys a chance to be a CO. It seems to me that you ought to accept it." Bruce's response left him unsatisfied, so the agent tried another approach.

"You have brothers and sisters at home, right?"

"Yes, I do," Bruce answered. He was the oldest of seven.

"What are they going to tell their friends at school when they are asked about their jailbird brother?"

Bruce was surprised by the use of such an emotional basis for persuasion, but he was sure of his answer.

"If I end up going to jail, they're going to understand why. I hope they'll understand it and maybe even be proud of it. If they don't, they don't, and they'll just have to work through that. If that's what's going to happen, that's what's going to happen."

The agent tried again. "Well, how is your mother going to take it? What will her friends say when they ask, 'How's Bruce?' and she has to say, 'My son is in jail'?"

Bruce simply repeated the response he had given earlier.

After using that line of argument several more times, the agent sighed heavily, and decided to try one last time. "Now look, son. Religious principles are nice to have—" And as he paused briefly to take a breath, Bruce interrupted.

"Pardon me, sir, but they really aren't." Bruce was looking intently at the agent, straight into his eyes. For the first and only time, he felt a flicker of recognition and understanding from the man.

"Oh," the agent said, and he stopped. Probably he had been planning to say that religious principles are nice things to have but there comes a time when you just have to be realistic and put them aside. Bruce had interrupted that chain of thought and maybe given him something new to think about.

Not having anything more to ask, the agent dismissed

him, saying that Bruce likely would be hearing from the FBI again.

"When?" Bruce asked. "Do you know what you're going to do?"

"No, we really don't know yet. But I'm sure you'll hear from us again soon," the agent repeated.

Walking away from the interview, Bruce felt okay. He could not think of anything he would have done or said differently. That evening he talked it over with a few students he knew but he began to feel quite alone; his closest friends were all somewhere else. They had not returned to EMC that fall, either because they had graduated or because their draft resistance had taken them elsewhere. Bruce missed all of them.

Contrary to the FBI agent's warning, Bruce had no further dealings with the FBI. But other worries weighed him down. He was isolated from the mainstream of college life. The previous year he had been an integral part of the student leadership group. The nagging pain of losing the student government presidency, combined with the absence of his closest friends, left him feeling lonely and dejected. As the school year waxed, he waned, feeling increasingly out of place and depressed. By the spring of 1971, he needed to get out of there. He went home to Ohio where he worked as a carpenter.

Being away from EMC was healing. By fall he felt ready to study again, and spent a semester at Cincinnati's Xavier University getting enough credits for an English degree from EMC.

In September 1972, he entered divinity school at Yale University. He hoped to gain a master's degree in religious studies and then perhaps pursue a doctorate in literature and theology. At Yale he met people with a wide range of religious experience. Their faith was a personal, vital response to an inner message. In that environment Bruce discovered more of his own unique gifts.

During his second year at Yale he met a priest, Doug Morrison, who was influential in changing Bruce's career plans. Father Morrison accepted Bruce fully, similar to the way Judy Parks had in Tennessee years before. Under his guidance, Bruce reached a tentative decision to explore the pastoral ministry.

His exploration led him into a variety of experiences—studying during a summer pastoral education program in New Haven, being an assistant minister at a Methodist church during his third year of studies, spending a summer in Atlantic City as a bar street minister, taking nine months of clinical pastoral education at a mental hospital near Baltimore. In all of this ministerial work, he gained a growing assurance that he should devote himself to the field of pastoring.

While working in the Baltimore area in 1976, he attended the Hyattsville Mennonite Church just outside of Washington, D.C. It was the first contact with Mennonites he had had since leaving EMC in 1971, and it felt good. The Hyattsville church welcomed Bruce's gifts of worship leading and preaching, and officially affirmed him with a commissioning service. The Mennonite Church, as embodied in the Hyattsville congregation, had recognized him as a minister. He now knew inside himself that he belonged with the Mennonite Church.

Discussions with a congregation in Richmond, Virginia, led to a position with them beginning in October 1976. From his base with the Richmond Mennonite Church, he has since gained recognition in the broader Mennonite Church as a frequent contributor of biblical meditations to various church magazines.

For Bruce, his draft resistance as a youth was not an isolated instance of peacemaking, nor was it part of a long-since dead fad of yesteryear. In the late 1970s he poured time and energy into an unsuccessful attempt to block the development of a military middle school in Richmond. When the draft registration was reactivated by Congress in 1980, he wrote letters to all the Mennonite pastors in the Virginia Mennonite Conference, urging their involvement in responding to the registration plans.

As with his draft resistance, though, his peacemaking continues to be more a personal act than a political one. Bruce's witness to peace is like a poem.

Epilogue

ennonites are sometimes said to be like cow manure. Clumped together on a dung heap, they give off a mighty smell; when scattered across the fields of the world, they do a lot of good fertilizing.

This book contains the stories of ten of the more than four dozen young Mennonites who resisted the Vietnam War by trying not to cooperate with the military conscription program. It could be said that these are the stories of people who left the manure pile of majority Mennonite experience. Or it could just as well be said that these are the stories of people who joined the manure pile of the non-Mennonite American counter-culture. But such analogies must be drawn with care, because they can easily buttress the widespread misunderstandings among Mennonites about Mennonite draft resisters of the 1960s and 1970s.

Many Mennonites thought that the resistance position had to mean that the resister considered himself better than someone who did not resist. Thus a dichotomy was set up: If one believed that the draft resisters were heroic fertilizers, one supposedly had to think that the manure pile stank. If, on the other hand, one believed that the manure pile smelled good and served a worthy purpose, one supposedly had to think that the draft resisters were heretical renegades. The contrast seemed unavoidable for many, and unfortunately it diverted attention away from the central issue of conscientious resistance. However, at many significant moments each side did show respect for the consciences of the other. Respect, of course, is something different from agreement, and that difference is perhaps what made the matter so controversial during the 1960s and 1970s.

The message of the draft resisters troubled the church to a degree that far outweighed their relatively small numbers. What appeared to be disturbing was that the draft resisters were drawing the line of conscientious objection at a point which was illegal. Their call for noncooperation with the Selective Service System meant that they felt their church's alternative service arrangements with the government were too much of a compromise for their consciences. The majority of Mennonites seemed upset both by the breaking of the law in principle and by the fact that a few resisters among them were saying that, at least for them, following conscience in their time could well incur suffering and that maybe the church should share in their suffering.

The concept of suffering runs deep in Mennonite identity. The martyrdom of thousands of early Anabaptists, the spiritual and cultural forebears of many modern Mennonites, is sacred history. In Mennonite life and thought, suffering and martyrdom have traditionally been open, visible signs of loyal, unswerving faith in Jesus Christ. There is thus an understandable inclination among Mennonites to jealously guard the martyrdom label, to make sure it is not cheapened in value by a watering down of its definition or even by it becoming too modern an event. Kept rare and unusual, martyrdom is a matter of pride. Kept distantly past, it is uncontroversial and nearly incapable of challenge or disrespect.

Another powerful motif among Mennonites has to do with what is called conscience. "Conscientious objector" is a holy phrase. Mennonites generally agree that following one's conscience before God is a necessary thing to do, even when, after much testing in the church fellowship, they may believe an

individual member's conscience is based on "an error of judgment," in the words of one articulate Mennonite opponent of
resistance to military conscription in the 1960s, Harold S.
Bender.[1]

Tremors of the debate were felt throughout the church.
The church periodicals occasionally carried news stories
about the draft resisters, as well as essays, editorials, and letters
on the pros and cons of draft resistance. The official
conference meetings of the various branches of Mennonites
were compelled to put the matter on their agenda and produce
statements. At issue was whether or not the church would officially say that noncooperation or other civil disobedience were
acceptable options with which its youth could respond to the
military conscription process. After much agonizing, the Mennonite Church at Turner, Oregon, in 1969, and the General
Conference Mennonite Church assembly at Fresno, California,
in 1971, gave hesitant approval to conscientious noncooperation. However, it is fair to question whether those statements
were representative of congregational conviction. Some congregations did give at least tacit approval to the consciences of
the noncooperators, most did not. Likewise, some church
leaders understood and supported the noncooperators, many
did not.

---

1. "When May Christians Disobey the Government?" January 12, 1960, *Gospel
Herald*.

The definition of conscience was at the heart of the debate over draft resistance in
the Mennonite church. Since one's conscience has to do with what one understands to
be right and good, the debate was over what actually is right and good. This may be
what made Vietnam-era resistance so confusing within the churches. Sometimes one
has to obey God and not cooperate with Caesar, the resisters would say. Yes, but not in
this instance, the mainstream of the church would reply.

In surveying the written records of the church debate, it appears that it was distorted by a certain style of argument. Although they rarely admitted it openly, each side seemed to assume the worst of reasons were behind the other's viewpoints. The resisters felt that others suspected their consciences were lacking in integrity. The question haunted them: Instead of true conscientious objection, was draft resistance not just pop anarchy, a militant rebellion against all authority, an immature attempt to be masochistic? On the other hand, those inclined to cooperate with the government and perform alternative service felt that the resisters suspected their consciences were lacking in integrity. The question haunted them: Instead of true conscientious objection, wasn't cooperating with Selective Service a faithless compromise, a selling of soul for mere privilege's sake?

While given to polarization and overstatement, the debate was probably worthwhile. It made individuals ask the crucial question: What do *I* believe? It forced a reevaluation of Mennonite identity and role in the world.

As sometimes happens in group history, the Mennonite "center" tried to put the new "fringe" of Mennonite draft resisters outside the boundary of what it meant to be Mennonite. Resistance is not Mennonite, said the center. It is the essence of our heritage, said the fringe.

The term "resistance" has indeed not been predominate in twentieth-century Mennonite history, and it has often been misunderstood because of the more familiar term, nonresistance. However, the number of occasions within that history where Mennonite conscientious objectors refused to comply with conscription is sufficient enough to merit a quick review. To object and be an objector, after all, is to resist something. What that "something" is has varied across eras and with individuals, but a common theme runs throughout.

About 2,000 Mennonites were conscripted during World War I. Nearly 10 percent of them were court-martialed and imprisoned for refusing to obey orders to do noncombatant work in the military camps. They did not all draw their line of conscientious objection at the same point. Some refused to follow all orders except to keep their own quarters tidy. Some accepted work only in the quartermaster or medical corps. Some accepted orders to clean up around the camp. Some refused to wear military clothing. Some fled the country to Canada.

A substantial number of the Mennonite resisters in World War I were subjected to severe punishment by the U.S. government:

> . . . they were bayoneted, beaten, and tortured by various forms of the water cure; eighteen men one night were aroused from their sleep and held under cold showers until one became hysterical. Another objector had the hose played upon his head until he became unconscious. . . . Men were forced to stand at attention, sometimes with outstretched arms for hours and days at a time on the sunny or cold side of their barracks, exposed to the inclemencies of the weather as well as to the jeers and taunts of their fellows until they could stand no longer; chased across the fields at top speed until they fell down exhausted, followed by their guards on motorcycles; occasionally tortured by mock trials, in which the victim was left under the impression to the very last that unless he submitted to the regulations the penalty would be death.[2]

Some of the resisters were given life sentences, a few were even sentenced to death. All of the sentences were later commuted, but two Hutterite Mennonites died as a result of mistreatment and ensuing illness.

2. *The Story of the Mennonites,* by C. H. Smith, Newton, Kansas, 1950, pp. 794-795.

The draft resistance debate of that time focused on the issue of noncombatant service under the direct supervision of the military. Was it consistent with Christian peacemaking? Guy F. Hershberger tells a story about how one of his Mennonite friends made up his mind on this matter of conscience.[3]

Just inducted, Hershberger's friend happened upon a group of soldiers being trained in bayonet practice. When one of the soldiers hesitated before he thrust his bayonet into the belly of the dummy victim, the drill sergeant swore loudly, reminding the timid private that they were engaged in a war, not a Sunday school picnic. His friend decided then and there that he would have nothing to do with any part of an organization that specialized in disemboweling human beings. He was later imprisoned for his refusal to obey orders.

During World War I, Lloy Kniss, later an eminent church leader in the Virginia Mennonite Conference, chose to resist by refusing to do most of the things he was ordered to do. His punishment ranged from being jeered at to being beaten.

"I objected to war and strife of any kind because of what Christ had meant to me in my life," he later wrote. "Noncombatant service . . . was also objectionable because the purpose was the same—to destroy the enemy.

"I had no desire to disobey anyone," Kniss explained. "But . . . my deep desire to obey God and my Christian conscience caused me to react in ways that I am sure must seem like sheer stubbornness."[4]

3. *War, Peace and Nonresistance* by Guy F. Hershberger, Scottdale, Pa.: Herald Press, 1969, pp. 116, 117.

4. *I Couldn't Fight: The Story of a C.O. in World War I* by Lloy Kniss, Scottdale, Pa.: Herald Press, 1971, pp. 5, 6, 25.

The draft experience in World War II differed markedly for Mennonites. Although Mennonites had made up a significant proportion of the total number of resisters during World War I, very few of the Mennonites conscripted in World War II resisted. A significant number of Mennonites who were not conscientious objectors accepted military service. And because the law had been changed, the Mennonites who were conscientious objectors found it easier to comply with the draft.

As a rule, young Mennonite conscientious objectors refused to cooperate with the World War II law only when for some unusual reason they were denied the new IV-E status. The IV-E classification exempted conscientious objectors from service in the military forces and required instead that they serve equivalent time in the newly created Civilian Public Service (CPS). Run by the churches, CPS was under the Selective Service System but without day-to-day military supervision.

Between 1941 and 1947, more than 4,600 Mennonites were assigned to CPS. They performed various tasks, initially in forestry, conservation, and park service work, later in agriculture, public health, and mental hospital work. There seems to be little record of any Mennonites who joined the hundreds of non-Mennonite conscientious objectors, called "absolutists," who resisted during this time. These people refused to cooperate with the draft law at the point of registration or induction, or they walked out of CPS camps because they felt that either the programs were too enmeshed in the military system or that churches should not be administering part of the military conscription program.

After World War II ended, the draft law was allowed to expire briefly. Then draft legislation was passed in 1948 that again provided for alternative service programs to be administered by the churches, but this time in a more decentralized fashion.

Most young Mennonite men registered under the new law and, when inductions were resumed in 1951, many followed the government's orders to perform alternative service in lieu of direct military work. But a few began to resist the 1948 law for reasons and in ways reminiscent of the World War I experiences.

Austin Regier, a Mennonite born in Kansas, had registered for the old draft law in the early 1940s and had served three years in Civilian Public Service. While in CPS camp, he became uneasy about his willing compliance with the conscription process that was feeding the war effort. He almost walked out but was persuaded by a Mennonite church leader to stay in CPS.

When Regier was discharged in 1946, he returned to Bethel College, the General Conference Mennonite college in Kansas, to complete his undergraduate studies, saying he would never again comply with the military draft system. Passage of the 1948 law made him put his words into practice. When he graduated that spring, he was 25 years old, little more than half a year away from being too old for the draft. Nevertheless, upon being ordered to register, he openly refused.

In the fall of 1948, Regier entered graduate school in economics. The FBI arrested him in November. In January 1949 he pleaded no contest and was sentenced to serve a year and a day in jail. He spent six months in federal prisons before he was paroled. In releasing him the parole officer registered him for the draft. Although Regier did not sign the form and refused to carry the draft cards, he never had any more trouble. Since 1956 he has been serving as a pastor in several United Methodist congregations in Michigan.

Another Mennonite at Bethel College also refused to register at about the same time as Regier. Dwight Platt turned

18 in 1949 and wrote a letter to President Truman and other officials explaining that he was resisting registration because it was part of the military program; he believed evil should be responded to with self-sacrifice, not violence. Platt was arrested in November 1950 and brought to trial in early 1951. Sentenced to a year and a day in jail, he served six months before he was paroled in late 1951.

The authorities registered Platt before he was released from prison, but he refused to carry his draft cards. For quite a while afterward, he tried to resist his draft board's attempts to classify and induct him. Finally he went overseas to India under the American Friends Service Committee and on its own the draft board allowed that unofficial assignment to satisfy his alternative service orders. Platt returned to join the faculty of Bethel College in the 1960s.

A third Mennonite at Bethel College resisted registration in 1949, having earlier served nineteen months in CPS during World War II. Ralph Bargen, a married student, was tried, convicted, and sentenced to prison for several months.

In another incident in the late 1950s, John W. Keim, a member of the Old Order Amish church, from Ashland, Ohio, registered but decided he would not go into alternative service when he was drafted. He reasoned that conscripted service at the order of the government would be a violation of his conscience against warmaking.

After he was drafted, Keim was sentenced to two years in jail, spending some of the time at a federal prison in Michigan and later as a prison trusty in Illinois, building a maximum security penitentiary at Marion. Keim had some very bad experiences in jail; at times he spent whole nights wide-awake fearing for his life. He was allowed to wear some of his distinctive Amish clothes while in prison, and he received much support from his home community.

Keim now runs a machine shop outside Ashland, Ohio. In response to the draft registration program begun in 1980, he said that he thinks he would not register this time if requested, and that he would be very open about his resistance with the government and his church. His younger brother, Albert Keim, also went to jail for draft resistance in the 1960s. Several other Amish from Ashland as well as Holmes County, Ohio, refused alternative service as a matter of conscience and were subsequently jailed during this period.

These incidents of draft resistance are but a few of the stories of noncooperation among Mennonites and Amish prior to the Vietnam War era. Their similarities to the resistance of Mennonites in the latter 1960s and early 1970s are more striking than their historically specific differences. In all, the objection was based on the conviction that there was a line across which they could not step and still preserve their conscience before God. That line always had to do with refusing to personally comply with the warring activities of the country. Also, it often was to serve as a witness against the godless purposes and actions of the military.

One of the most commonly heard complaints about Mennonite draft resisters in the Vietnam era was that they might make it more difficult for other Mennonites to maintain their privilege of alternative service. The same charge could have been (and perhaps was) applied to Lloy Kniss in World War I. His recalcitrance at taking orders could well have jeopardized the noncombatant CO privilege of hundreds of Mennonites who in conscience were able to perform medical and quartermaster functions for the military. Yet as the delegation of Mennonite leaders approached the White House to appeal for the alternative service exemption in the 1940s, the history of the World War I noncooperators' hardships moved the government to respond positively.

Another common criticism of Mennonite draft resistance during the Vietnam War era dismissed the resisters as mere products of their time. The surrounding culture of America's non-Mennonites does of course tend to shape the Mennonite peace agenda. But while it was generally unpopular by the early and mid-1970s, the Vietnam War enjoyed a broad-based mandate from the American public throughout much of the 1960s when many of the Mennonite draft resisters were making up their minds about their noncooperation. The charge that resistance was "just a fad" was generally reciprocal. In this case cooperation was as much a fad as noncooperation; conformity to the world could be laid at the feet of cooperators and resisters alike. Mennonite resisters of all times have tried to rebuff such false characterizations of their intent and character. Their sincerity is made somewhat more credible because some of the resisters have had to pay dearly for their beliefs. Fads fade in the face of hardship, convictions remain firm.

For Mennonite conscientious objectors, noncooperation can be as valid an option as alternative service. In Mennonite history, the patterns of noncooperation have varied with individuals and historical contexts. But the principle has remained unchanged—there comes a time when a conscientious objector cannot cooperate with a requirement to participate in the military system. At some points in history, such beliefs leave one with no easy way out. They often lead one to take the path of most resistance.

So how does one decide whether the Vietnam-era Mennonite draft resisters were heroes or heretics? Perhaps the dichotomy is drawn too sharply for real humans in real situations on an issue of personal conscience. The preceding ten stories seem to indicate that this is the case.

Authors' Note

Interviewing these ten men and their families and friends was a moving experience for both them and us. Many of the people we talked with had stored away intense emotions in their memories, and these emotions came tumbling out in the process of recalling the past.

Several different things became clear to us in researching this book. It must have been painfully difficult for many Mennonites in those times to discern what was right and what was wrong. Mothers and fathers, sons and their girlfriends, college administrators and church officials, all expressed a degree of ambivalence in reflecting on their actions and the reasoning behind them.

Another vivid impression that we were left with was the youthfulness of the resisters. At eighteen, twenty, or twenty-two many of these young men were making life decisions that held the potential for serious, long-term consequences.

We wondered how the resisters' earlier experiences would affect their adult life. In being interviewed a decade later, the resisters seemed to recognize that they had survived some traumatic experiences which, they said for the most part, were good for them to have gone through. Many of them recounted their resistance experiences with a great deal of humbleness, often saying, "Aren't there more important stories to tell?" They expressed concern for future generations of conscientious objectors, saying that they were willing to have their stories included in this book if that could help someone else work through their beliefs and decisions. This is our hope as well.

Appendix A
Mennonite Church 1969
Statement on Draft Resistance

*The following statement and response
was endorsed by the delegates attending the
General Conference session (later denoted
as "General Assembly") of the Mennonite
Church meeting at Turner, Oregon, August
18, 1969.*

W e are grateful that a group of young people have
come to this Mennonite General Conference session
at considerable personal sacrifice to speak their Christian convictions regarding the evils of conscription. We have received
the following message from them:

A Brief Statement on Mennonite Draft Resistance

The Mennonite Church, throughout its history, has held
the doctrine of nonresistance as central to its interpretation of
the Christian faith. The practical application of nonresistance
by the church has taken various forms historically, and has
been met with varied responses by the nation-state.
Mennonites in the United States presently experience

very little, if any, difficulty in the area of military service. The Selective Service System has given us an opportunity to fulfill our service obligation without directly becoming members of the military.

A small, but growing number of Mennonite young people find the present arrangement with the United States government totally unacceptable. The Vietnam War and the continued military conscription have prompted us to examine our individual and church relationships with the Selective Service System. By cooperating with this agency we, in effect, are sanctioning its actions.

We are also disturbed by the pervasiveness of militarism and militaristic thought in the United States. In the spirit of what we hope is a prophetic witness both to the church and the state, we feel an obligation as Christians to resist these tendencies.

Selective Service System must be considered an integral part of the military. Its only purpose is to channel men into various vocations related directly or indirectly to killing. This channeling of men necessarily involves coercion and therefore interferes with Christian vocation as we understand it.

Christian service and a witness of peace cannot be coerced. They must be spontaneous in nature, and motivated by Christian love and concern for the individual and society.

It is for these basic reasons that we willfully refuse to cooperate with the Selective Service System. We feel that this is the stance we have to assume as Christians. We do not attempt to willfully rebel against the state, but recognize that our first loyalty and obedience is to God.

We do not advocate that the Mennonite Church should officially state that noncooperation is the practice it will now assume. Certainly we accept the existing arrangements as being viable for those unable to agree with, or accept the position of total noncooperation.

We feel that God is calling the church to move in a new direction of prophetic witness. With this in mind, we submit the following proposals to the Mennonite Church for consideration and action.

Response to Conscription and Militarism

In response to this statement we (the Mennonite Church) take the following action:

1. We reaffirm our position statements of the Mennonite General Conference made in 1937 and 1951 with regard to peace, war, military service, and positive Christian service according to the church's interpretation of the life and teachings of Christ.

2. We renew our efforts to educate the youth of the Mennonite Church in our historic nonresistant faith.

3. We ask the Committee on Peace and Social Concerns and the MCC Peace Section to examine closely our present policy of cooperation with the Selective Service System.

4. *We recognize the validity of noncooperation as a legitimate witness and pledge the offices of our brotherhood to minister to young men in any eventuality they incur in costly discipleship.*

5. We instruct our counseling agencies to work more closely in assisting young men who have chosen to migrate to another country for conscience sake.

6. We ask the service organizations of the church to express a willingness to accept individuals into service programs who cannot conscientiously cooperate with the Selective Service System.

7. We increase our draft counseling programs both to Mennonites and non-Mennonites.

8. We continue to support church-related alternate service as a legitimate option for those who do not feel called to a position of noncooperation. Even though some consider such service a compromise in our witness against war, we will support anyone who is willing to affirm the preservation and enrichment of life over the destruction of life by accepting an alternative service assignment.

9. We commend to our brotherhood the position of Christian service as vocation not only for men conscripted by Selective Service, but also for those young men of draft age not conscripted, for young women, and for persons of all ages.

10. We counsel our brotherhood to respect civil authority, to obey it in all areas where it does not violate conscience, and to reject the spirit of violence of our age.

> Mennonite General Conference
> Turner, Oregon
> August 18, 1969

Appendix B
General Conference Mennonite Church 1971 Statement on Draft Resistance

The following resolution of the General Conference Mennonite Church (excerpted from pages 16 and 17 of "A Christian Way of Peace") was adopted at its triennial session at Fresno, California, in August 1971.

... The way of peace applied to conscription and military service.

Conscription for military service is a means by which modern nations are able to wage war. We therefore will work for the termination of conscription or any involuntary recruitment program.

As Christians desiring to follow the Jesus way of love, we cannot accept service in any military organization, either in combatant or noncombatant position. This applies to all wars, whether designated defensive or offensive.

Wherever and whenever conscription exists, we will encourage draft-age youth to enter some form of meaningful alternative service program. Under the lordship of Christ, we claim the right of conscientious objection to war. We appreciate the legal provision governments make for recognition of this right. Where governments have not acknowledged this right we call on them to do so. As a church we shall continue to provide channels for Christian service both at home and abroad, and will encourage our youth to witness for peace in these church programs. Youth who desire to participate in an alternative service program are encouraged to seek positions which identify with the suffering in the world and thereby seek to prevent violence and war.

Affirming the priesthood of all believers, we recommend that Christians not make use of ministerial exemption to avoid alternative obligations.

Some of our brotherhood see cooperation with conscription as contrary to Christian discipleship. Since conscription helps make it possible to wage war, it is important to question whether this is a proper function of governments and to discern what response faithfulness to Christ asks of us. *We recognize noncooperation with the military draft when based on loyalty to Jesus as a valid witness. We pledge the resources of our brotherhood to a supportive ministry to young men who take such a stand. We ask our counseling and service agencies to work closely with young men who have chosen to migrate to another country or who suffer imprisonment as a witness against militarism. . . .*

The Authors

Melissa Miller lives in Waterloo, Ontario, with her husband, Dean Peachey, where she works part-time as Youth Minister for the Mennonite Conference of Ontario, and as an intern at Interfaith Pastoral Counseling Centre in Kitchener, Ontario.

Miller received her BA degree in psychology in 1976 from Eastern Mennonite College, Harrisonburg, Virginia. She received a master's degree in applied psychology from the University of Waterloo in 1981. She has taught psychology at Eastern Mennonite College, worked with mentally handicapped adults, and conducted community and playground activities with children.

Born in Roaring Spring, Pennsylvania, Miller was a member of the Church of the Brethren until joining Mannheim Mennonite Church in Mannheim, Ontario.

U ntil 1981 Phil M. Shenk was on the editorial staff of *So-journers,* a magazine published by a Christian community church in inner-city Washington, D.C. He is now a full-time law student at Catholic University, also in Washington, D.C.

Shenk received a BS degree in the liberal arts in 1979 from Eastern Mennonite College, Harrisonburg, Virginia, after having suspended his formal academic studies for several years. Prior to this he was a founding participant in the college's Study-Service Year program in Washington.

Between 1977 and 1979, Shenk served as a professional staff member under U.S. Senator James Abourezk, chairman of the Senate Select Committee on Indian Affairs, with a focus on resolving problems in native American Indian housing and education programs run by the government.

Born in Lancaster, Pennsylvania, Shenk is a member of Erisman Mennonite church, near Manheim, Pennsylvania. He moved to Washington, D.C., in 1976 where he became active in the Mennonite Student and Young Adult Services program, and deeply involved in the life and worship activities of Sojourners Fellowship.